P9-BYS-429

Noah's Flood

# Noah's Flood

*The Genesis Story in Western Thought*

Norman Cohn

Yale University Press
New Haven & London

Copyright © 1996 by Norman Cohn

All rights reserved. This book may not be reproduced in whole or in part, in any form (beyond that copying permitted by Sections 107 and 108 of the U.S. Copyright Law and except by reviewers for the public press) without written permission from the publishers.

Set in New Baskerville by Best-set Typesetter Ltd, Hong Kong
Printed in Hong Kong through World Print Ltd

Library of Congress Cataloging-in-Publication Data
Cohn, Norman Rufus Colin.
    Noah's flood: the Genesis story in Western thought/Norman Cohn.
    Includes bibliographical references and index.
    ISBN 0-300-06823-9 (alk. paper)
    1. Deluge—History of doctrines.   I. Title.
  BS658.C64   1996
  222′.1106′09—dc20                                          96–18500
                                                                CIP

A catalogue record for this book is available from the British Library.

10 9 8 7 6 5 4 3 2 1

*Frontispiece*: Animals entering the ark. From a French Book of Hours, *c.* 1470.

For Vera

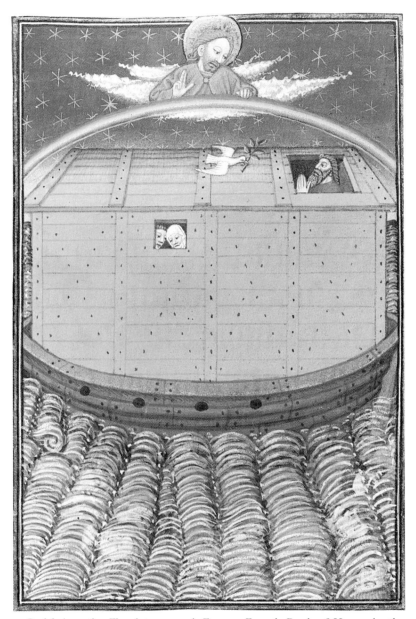

1 God brings the Flood to an end. From a French Book of Hours, by the Fastolf Master, *c.* 1440–50.

# Contents

Illustration Acknowledgements     ix

Foreword     xi

Acknowledgements     xiii

1   Mesopotamian Origins     1

2   The Genesis Story     11

3   Hidden Meanings     23

4   Filling Gaps     32

5   A Ruined Earth     47

6   Providential Comets     62

7   Problematic Fossils     73

8   Shifting Time-Scales     94

9   Harmonizers     109

10   Fundamentalists     121

11   Hidden Meanings Again     130

Appendix     134

Notes     138

Index     151

# Illustration Acknowledgements

The Walters Art Gallery, Baltimore: frontispiece; The Bodleian Library, Oxford: 1 (MS. Auct. D. inf. 2.11. f. 59v); National Museum, Warsaw: 2; The British Library, London: 3 (Cotton Nero CIV f. 3), 13, 14 (Add. MSS. 11695 f. 79v), 15, 17, 20, 22, 23, 26, 28, 29, 30, 31; Photo Scala, Florence: 4, 5, 10; Photo Alinari, Florence: 6, 25; © Arch. Phot. Paris/DACS 1996: 9; Prado, Madrid/Bridgeman Art Library, London: 11; Victoria and Albert Museum/Bridgeman Art Library London; 16; by courtesy of the Governors of Sutton's Hospital in Charterhouse/Photo Eileen Tweedy: 18; National Portrait Gallery, London: 21; copyright Royal Society: 24; Sedgwick Museum, University of Cambridge: 27; Scottish National Portrait Gallery, Edinburgh: 32; The Metropolitan Museum of Art, Gift of William Merrit Chase, 1909: 33; Yale Center for British Art: 34; Department of Geology, University of Oxford: 35; Museum of the History of Science, University of Oxford: 36; The Maas Gallery, London/Bridgeman Art Library, London: 37.

2  *Noah's Ark*, by Roelant Savery of Utrecht (1576–1639).

# Foreword

Stories about a universal flood have been found in many parts of the world – in fact some three hundred such stories have been recorded.[1] Various interpretations of this mass of material have been advanced by anthropologists, folklorists and geologists. This book, however, is concerned with only one flood: Noah's.

The story of Noah's Flood, as told in Genesis, has of course inspired painters, sculptors, poets, dramatists, composers. That it has also, century after century, stimulated a great deal of hard thinking is not generally recognised. My aim has been to consider, firstly, how the story originated and how it acquired its peculiar resonance; and then to examine what later thinkers have made of it.

As, over some two thousand years, western beliefs and values have been transformed again and again, those mutations have been mirrored in the ever-changing interpretations which have been put upon this simple tale. Emerging from a Mesopotamian experiment in royal and priestly propaganda, the story of Noah's Flood became for Jews a message of consolation and hope, for Christians a prefiguring of salvation. Later it changed, for Jews and Christians alike, into an excuse for extravagant flights of fancy and strenuous exercises in pedantry. From the seventeenth to the nineteenth century it was deeply involved in the development of scientific geology, which it both furthered and impeded. From the late eighteenth century to the present day it has been involved also in the conflict between traditional religious beliefs and science, and in the efforts to reconcile the two. Deprived of all plausibility by the discovery of geological time, for fundamentalists it has nevertheless remained literally and demonstrably true. Has any other story in all the world had such a varied career?

As I at last, in my eighty-second year, take leave of Noah's Flood, I recall the words of an American scholar, written some thirty-five years ago:

> . . . knowledge for its own sake is not enough; one must let one's mind grow through seeing the minds of men at work through recurrent time. In this Noah story we surely see this very thing – the genuinely working minds of highly primitive and highly sophisticated men – vivid and eager, full of *hubris* and full of persistence, imaginative, solid, fanciful, reasoning, breaking closed systems, full of error and of truth. The Noah story, sensibly used, can bring the man who wants to know something of culture change, and of the permanence of culture, to a number of contrasting cultures . . .[2]

I can think of no better way of explaining why it seemed worth my while to study this subject and to write this book.

Wood End
Hertfordshire, England

# Acknowledgements

Not for the first time, I have cause to congratulate myself on having Yale University Press as my publisher. *Noah's Flood* owes much to Robert Baldock for his thoughtful and helpful suggestions; to Candida Brazil for the scrupulous care with which she prepared the text for publication; and to Sheila Lee for the zeal and skill with which she tracked down the illustrations.

My wife Vera and my son Nik patiently read and re-read early drafts of the book. But for their penetrating and constructive criticisms, the finished product would be far more imperfect than it is.

3  Building the ark. The ark rides the Flood, while mankind drowns. From the thirteenth-century Psalter of Henri de Blois.

# Chapter 1

## Mesopotamian Origins

1

The story of the Flood, which we know from Genesis and associate with Noah, originated in Mesopotamia.

Right down to the first half of the present century large areas of what used to be Mesopotamia and is now Iraq were frequently devastated by flood. When torrential rain combined with the melting of the snows in spring, the Tigris and the Euphrates could burst their banks; then the country would be submerged under hundreds of miles of lake. In ancient times this phenomenon gave rise to a powerful tradition: it was believed that there had once been a flood so overwhelming that nothing was ever the same again. In the famous Sumerian king-list the kings are even divided into two categories, ante-diluvian and post-diluvian.

It may well be that the tradition reflected, however distortedly, a real event. Excavations indicate that around 2800 BCE the ancient Sumerian city of Shurrupak (now Tell Fara), about 30 km north of Uruk, was laid waste by a flood[1] – and of the three major flood stories that are preserved in writing, one refers to Shurrupak by name, while in another the chief protagonist bears the name of a king of Shurrupak who is known to have reigned around the time of that catastrophe.[2] The earliest of these writings is a fragment of a Sumerian poem from the temple library of the ancient city of Nippur;[3] and though the tablet on which it is inscribed dates from around 1600 BCE, it is likely that the story it tells had been circulating, as oral folklore, for a thousand years before that.

It seems that in the original text the story of the Flood was simply one episode in a history of mankind. The surviving fragment opens with the last part of a speech delivered by a god – obviously the supreme god Enlil – to an assembly of gods. The speaker tells how he established the divine laws; established kingship by sending it down from heaven to earth; established five Sumerian cities, gave them names and set a ruler over each; and established the irrigation on which all Sumer depended. Then comes a lacuna: the text here evidently reported how the gods decided to send the Flood and wipe out mankind. As the surviving text resumes we learn how some of the deities, including the goddess Inanna, wept for the people. And we meet a pious king called Ziusdra or Ziusudra, who is humbly seeking a revelation from the gods.

Revelation is granted. Standing close to a wall, Ziusdra hears the voice of a god and learns of the decision of the divine assembly: a flood will sweep over the cities and 'the seed of mankind' will perish. And a word from the three highest deities will overthrow the kingship too.

After a further lacuna we learn how Ziusdra survives storm and flood in a huge vessel (doubtless built according to divine instructions):

> All the destructive winds [and] gales were present,
> The storm swept over the capitals.
> After the storm had swept the country for seven days
>     and seven nights
> And the destructive winds had rocked the huge boat
>     in the high water,
> The Sun came out, illuminating the earth and sky,
> Ziusdra made an opening in the huge boat.
> The king Ziusdra
> Prostrated himself before the Sun god,
> The king slaughtered a large number of bulls and sheep.

After which Ziusdra prostrates himself before the highest gods, who grant him 'eternal life, like a god' as a reward for having preserved 'the seed of mankind'. Finally Ziusdra is settled in a supernatural realm, Dilmun.

This Sumerian version of the Flood story seems to have been composed for a political purpose: to strengthen the established order. The king was central to that order – and the story not only insists that kingship was established by the gods (something that every Sumerian knew well enough) but also shows us a king who was so devoted to the gods that they rewarded him with safe conduct during the Flood and immortality after it. Closely linked with the king were the priests – and the poem is concerned with their interests too. In the opening speech before the assembly of gods, Enlil announces that after the destruction of 'my human race' he wishes the survivors to build new cities 'on holy places' and to work for the observance and promotion of the divine laws. In all this one seems to hear the voice of a court poet.

When, towards 1800 BCE, the Semite Hammurabi founded the Babylonian empire, which included Sumer, much of Sumerian religion and literature was adopted – and adapted – by the conquerors. The Flood story in particular was taken up and rewritten, modified and elaborated, in Akkadian.

The most significant of these writings is an Old Babylonian poem commonly known as the *Atrahasis Epic*. The best available copy, which is in the British Museum, dates from around 1635 BCE, but the original text may have been written down a century or two earlier. The part which deals with the Flood can usefully be supplemented by Tablet XI of the famous *Epic of Gilgamesh*, which is clearly based on a version of the same story.[4]

In *Atrahasis* the story of the Flood is preceded by an account of how human beings first came into existence and how they brought divine wrath down on themselves. Originally the lesser gods performed the labour necessary to maintain the world, especially irrigating the marshes. Their labour also provided sustenance for the greater gods. But after some forty years of back-breaking work the lesser gods revolted and downed tools – in fact burned their tools. Then they went and surrounded the house of the chief of the gods, Enlil, whose particular domain was the earth.

Enlil was asleep, so did not notice what was happening. Woken up, he could think of nothing better than to summon an assembly of the gods. In particular he turned for advice to the god Enki, who ruled over the fresh waters underground and who was also noted for his wiliness and ingenuity. Enki rose to the occasion: he proposed the creation of a new being, man, to take over the work of the lesser gods. And with the help of the mother goddess Nintu this was carried out: man was created out of a mixture of clay and the flesh and blood of a slain god. So human beings were brought into being to act as the servants, if not the slaves, of the gods. It was a notion which had long been standard amongst the peoples of Mesopotamia.

Unfortunately the solution proved to be only a temporary one. Before 1,200 years had elapsed human beings had become so numerous that their noise disturbed the gods. Just when Enlil wanted to sleep, 'the land bellowed like a bull'. First Enlil tried to deal with the problem by persuading the gods to send plague – which effectively reduced the population and so the noise. However, after a further 1,200 years the population and the noise were back where they had been. This time rain was withheld, to some effect. But still the problem recurred and after another 1,200 years Enlil was again being kept awake. Outraged, the gods combined to withhold both rain and the yearly inundation for six successive years, with horrifying results: reduced to starvation, neighbours fell upon one another, parents killed and devoured their own children.

On both occasions salvation came from Enki. The wily god meant well by the species he had brought into being and was increasingly alienated from the gods who were set upon destroying it. So as Enlil devised one genocidal plan after another, Enki thwarted it. For Enki had a devotee, one Atrahasis: the name meant 'exceedingly wise one'. Atrahasis was a mythical king, whose reign was imagined as lasting throughout the entire span covered by the story, 4,800 years. As each catastrophe threatened, this devout man prayed for help to his patron god, and each time Enki responded. Thanks to Enki's various interventions mankind survived, to multiply as vigorously as before.

Finally Enlil decided to send a flood which would altogether annihilate mankind. This time the gods had to swear not to tell any mortal of the plan – but Enki found a way round that too: he passed the information not directly to Atrahasis but to the wall of the reed hut where he lived, and the wall – perhaps thanks to the wind whistling through it – transmitted the message.

Enki's advice was to build a huge boat and coat it with pitch; according to the *Epic of Gilgamesh*, he was to pull down his hut and build a boat from the reeds (reed boats were as common as reed huts).[5] Atrahasis set about the task with a will. As king he had to account for this strange behaviour to a council of elders; for their benefit he explained that, as Enlil and Enki had fallen out, he could no longer live on Enlil's earth but must sail away to join his patron god in the waters beneath the earth. So he was left in peace to build his boat – which, as *Gilgamesh* makes clear, was more like a house: a gigantic cube, the size of a ziggurat, with seven levels, each divided into seven compartments. Atrahasis was allowed only seven days in which to construct his new abode, but with the help of well-fed labourers he managed it. Then he loaded it with his possessions, gold and silver, and with animals and birds; and again Enki helped, by raining down an abundance of loaves and wheat. Before embarking, Atrahasis gave a banquet – but was unable to enjoy it, because of his horror at the impending catastrophe.

The gods took an active part in the Flood which then swept across the earth. The storm-god Adad rumbled inside the black clouds, other gods made the dikes overflow, others again lifted their torches and set the land ablaze. Everything was turned to blackness, the mountains disappeared under water, the people were all drowned. The pounding storm, the raging flood were like a war. The gods themselves were terrified, crouching and cowering like dogs, and struggling to escape from the earth to the sky. Deprived of the offerings of food and drink on which they depended, they mourned the destruction of mankind; with burning lips and parched throats they sat, humbly weeping and sobbing. And the mother-goddess reproached herself bitterly for having consented to the catastrophe that had destroyed her people.

Atrahasis' boat rode out the storm until, after seven days and nights, it came to rest on a mountain. Then Atrahasis looked out and saw the land flattened like a roof, and all human beings turned to clay. For another week he waited, while the boat remained lodged on the mountain-top. Then he sent out a dove, but the dove, finding no perch, returned. The same happened when a swallow was sent out. But by the time a raven was sent out, the waters were receding, the bird was able to scratch the earth and eat, so it stayed away. Then Atrahasis came out of the boat, sacrificed a sheep and burned incense; the gods, smelling the savour, gathered round 'like flies'. As for Enlil, at first he was furious that any human being at all had survived – but then he had to endure the reproaches of the mother-goddess and of Enki for the thoughtlessness with which he had condemned mankind to annihilation.

Mankind had indeed survived – and the long-standing problem remained. But again Enki found a solution: henceforth some women would be barren, from others a demon would snatch their babies away; and there were to be institutions for religious women who would be forbidden to marry. So overpopulation would be permanently forestalled.[6]

The author of the *Atrahasis Epic* clearly thinks well of mankind, poorly of almost all the gods. This is not a story about sin and its consequences. Although Mesopotamians were familiar with the notion of sin, it is not sin that precipitates the Flood. The offence of human beings is simply that they multiply and, as a result, make too much noise for the gods' comfort. That such a slight and unwitting offence evokes such a lethal response is due to the shortcomings of the gods: they are tyrants – and stupid tyrants at that. If the gods were less stupid, if they had the slightest capacity for foresight and rational planning, they would have borne in mind their total dependence on mankind. For had not human beings been created precisely because the gods could not provide for themselves?

The chief god Enlil cuts a particularly sorry figure. He is supposed to be a mighty leader, yet when the lesser gods besiege his house he has to call first on the assembly of the gods and then on Enki to deal with the situation. And when human beings in their turn produce new problems, Enlil's reaction is at first ineffective, and later so imprudent that the very survival of the gods is called in question. But the criticism directed against Enlil involves almost all the gods. For – as the mother-goddess points out – the whole assembly of the gods consented to the Flood. The picture that the poet paints of the gods when faced with the consequences – how they suffer thirst and hunger pangs, and how later they

swarm about Atrahasis' offerings – makes them look both con-
temptible and ridiculous. Only Enki is exempt: he alone foresees
problems and solves them when they arise.

What lies behind this critique? The Old Babylonian period
witnessed the development of an institution which was without
parallel in earlier periods of Mesopotamian history: the 'tablet-
house'.[7] This was a sort of university where junior scribes were
trained by senior scribes to become both scholars and secretaries
of state. These scribes could and did make intellectual revolutions
by demoting and promoting gods. And as the only true intellectuals in that society, indeed the only literate individuals, they will
naturally have felt a particular kinship with Enki, whose potency
lay not in brute strength but in his subtle intelligence. This is no
mere guess. In the famous epic *Enuma elish* a new god called Nabu
appears, divine patron and prototype of scribes and secretary to
the god Marduk, who himself had just been promoted to supreme
rule over the cosmos: clearly a projection into the cosmos of
the scribes' self-image. In *Atrahasis* Enki profits from the same
predilection.

But if the gods as a collectivity are demoted in *Atrahasis*, a
moderate solace is offered to mankind. Barrenness in women, the
deaths of babies are of course grievous afflictions, and celibate
priestesses could be thought of as useless. Nevertheless, in
*Atrahasis* these things are presented as necessary and good:
through them the potentially ruinous fertility of human beings is
brought under control. They were, after all, innovations of Enki's
– and Enki is, unfailingly, the friend of mankind.

Thanks to these devices, human beings can rest assured that the
Flood will never return. In the post-diluvian world the disorder of
the ante-diluvian world cannot recur, nor that false remedy. A
stable balance has been established on earth – and the gods, for
their part, have learned their lesson.


### 2


The Mesopotamian story of the Flood spread far and wide in
the ancient world. The Babylonian version was known to the
Canaanites – in fragments found at the Canaanite city of Ras

Shamra the hero still bears the name Atrahasis. Fragments of the story have also been found on tablets from the royal library of the Hittites at Boghasköy, in central Turkey. It seems to have been the Hittites, too, who transmitted the story to the Greeks – there were Greek colonies along the coast of Asia Minor at the time when Asia Minor belonged to the Hittite empire.

For Greeks the story had in fact a special appeal, for they too had experienced a mighty flood. In the days of Deucalion, who reigned over part of Thessaly about the middle of the fifteenth century BCE, the volcano Santorin in the Aegean sea erupted and collapsed. This must have caused such colossal seismic waves that large areas of mainland Greece would have been devastated.[8] Memories of such a catastrophe survived for many centuries – Aristotle and Plato both refer to a great deluge which occurred in the days of Deucalion and his wife Pyrrha – so it is not surprising that the Mesopotamian flood story found a ready audience. In the second century BCE the Greek writer Apollodorus produced a brief summary of it, in which all the features of the original were preserved, though skilfully adapted to Greek culture. Here too the survivors are identified as Deucalion and Pyrrha.

The story was transmitted by the Greeks to the Romans. Ovid, writing in Rome at the very end of the first century BCE, has left a notable version.[9] Once upon a time Jupiter, from his lofty throne, observed the evil deeds of human beings – their contempt for the gods, their violence, their lust for slaughter. Furious, the supreme god summoned a council of the gods and announced his decision: mankind must be exterminated, lest men turn their violence against the demigods inhabiting the earth – the nymphs and fauns and satyrs.

Jupiter also reported how he himself had wandered the earth, to check whether human beings were really as wicked as it seemed. Though the common people had been willing enough to worship him when they realised that he was a god, he had been monstrously insulted: King Lycaon had killed a man, cooked his flesh and set it on the table before him. Jupiter had punished Lycaon at once by turning him into a wolf; but he also resolved to wipe mankind off the face of the earth. The gods were grieved to hear it. What state would the earth be in without mortals, they asked, and who would bring incense to their altars? Jupiter reassured them – he would provide another race of beings, of wondrous origin, and far superior to the first.

How to proceed? Jupiter thought of hurling his thunderbolts at the earth, but then, mindful of the prophecy that in the end the whole universe will be destroyed by fire, stayed his hand. Instead, he let the south wind loose, to pour down rain, set the sea god Triton to produce huge waves, and bade the rivers overflow their dikes and loose their fountains. The result was that most of mankind was drowned, and the rest slowly starved to death. Other forms of life fared no better.

Only Deucalion and Pyrrha were saved. There was no better man than Deucalion, none more concerned to live aright. No woman revered the gods more devoutly than Pyrrha. They were forewarned by Prometheus, built a ship, loaded it with provisions, and were borne to Mount Parnassus, the only spot not covered by the waters. Disembarking, they worshipped the nymphs and the mountain deities and great Themis, the goddess who kept the oracles that foretold men's fate. Then Jupiter quieted the storm and Triton blew his conch shell to make the waters retreat.

The earth was empty of human beings, and Deucalion and Pyrrha wept to think that the future of mankind depended on them alone. So they went to Themis' shrine and asked how their race might be restored. She had her answer ready: they must go forth and, with veiled heads and loosened robes, throw behind them as they walked the bones of their great mother. The two were mystified – until Deucalion divined that those bones must be the stones in the earth's body. So they did as they were told, and the stones that they threw gradually took on human form; Deucalion's stones becoming men, Pyrrha's becoming women. As for other forms of life, the earth produced them spontaneously.

Down to the second century CE the story of the Flood continued to circulate in the Hellenistic world in versions that were clearly derived from the Mesopotamian tradition and quite unrelated to the account in Genesis.[10] However, it was through the Genesis version that the story acquired the vitality which has carried it down the centuries, right to our own times.

4  Building the ark. Noah introduces the animals and his family into the ark. Mosaic, San Marco, Venice, twelfth-century.

# Chapter 2

## *The Genesis Story*

1

The biblical story of the Flood is recounted in four chapters (6–9) of the Book of Genesis.[1] In outline the story is as familiar as any in the world. Many of the details, on the contrary, tend nowadays to be ignored. Yet in the past those same details exerted endless fascination and stimulated a vast amount of speculation. A brief summary may not come amiss.

Ten generations, we are told, had passed since God set Adam upon the newly created earth, and mankind had become very wicked: human beings were wholly given over to planning and doing evil. And other creatures had transgressed most grievously:

> The earth was corrupt in the view of God, and it was full of lawlessness. And God saw how corrupt the earth was, for all flesh had corrupted their ways on earth.[2]

When God considered the state of the world he found it so spoiled by its inhabitants that he was sorry to have created such beings at all.

One righteous man there was – the 600-year-old Noah, who 'walked with God' and was 'without blame in that age'. To him alone God confided his intention: 'I am about to bring on the Flood . . . to eliminate everywhere all flesh in which there is the breath of life: everything on earth shall perish.'[3] And God gave

Noah precise instructions. He was to build a wooden ark (the Hebrew word means 'chest' or 'box') and cover it inside and out with pitch. The ark was to be 300 cubits in length, fifty cubits in breadth, thirty cubits in height. (A cubit equals approximately a foot and a half.) It was to have a roof, three decks divided into compartments, a door in its side, and a window. As soon as it was finished Noah and his wife and their three sons and the sons' wives were to go into it, and they were to take with them a pair of every kind of bird, mammal and reptile. Enough provisions were to be stored inside the ark, of every appropriate kind, to keep everyone alive.

Noah did as he was commanded and God shut the door of the ark behind him. Then 'all the fountains of the great deep burst forth, and the sluices in the sky broke open'.[4] It rained, until the flood rose high above the earth's surface, in fact fifteen cubits above the top of the highest mountains. The ark drifted on the surface of the waters. Meanwhile, 'all flesh that had stirred on earth perished – birds, cattle, beasts, all the creatures that swarmed on earth and all mankind . . . they were blotted out from the earth. Only Noah was left, and those that were with him in the ark.'[5]

The Flood lasted a long time – according to one account in Genesis, 101 days, according to another, a full solar year – but in the end God remembered Noah and his companions in the ark and decided to bring the cataclysm to an end. Gradually the waters receded, until the ark came to rest on the mountains of Ararat. After a long wait the mountain-crests came into sight. Again Noah waited, until it seemed right to send out a raven to reconnoitre. The raven flew to and fro, waiting for the water to dry off from the earth, but did not return to the ark. So a dove was sent out; being a more domesticated creature, when it found nowhere to settle it returned, and Noah took it back into the ark. Sent out again a week later, the dove again returned, this time with a plucked olive leaf in its beak; so Noah knew that the waters had subsided. Sent out a third time, the dove stayed away, showing that the earth was dry. On God's instructions Noah and his family came out of the ark, and the other creatures followed them out.

5   The story of the Flood, from the mass drowning to the happy ending for Noah, his family and the saved animals. Mosaic, San Marco, Venice, twelfth-century.

Next Noah built an altar and sacrificed burnt offerings on it. This he was able to do because God, foreseeing such a situation, had ordered that additional animals and birds of the kinds used for sacrifice should be taken into the ark. When God smelled the odour of the burnt offering he swore to himself that, irretrievably evil though human beings were, he would never again curse the earth because of man, nor would he ever again destroy all living creatures. There would be no further cataclysm: 'Never again shall all flesh be cut off by the waters of the flood; neither shall there be another flood to devastate the earth.'[6] It was the opening of a new era, the post-diluvian age. The way this emergence of a new world is presented recalls – and was certainly intended to recall – the original creation of the world.

To inaugurate the new world, God established a covenant not only with Noah and his descendants but with all living creatures, every beast and bird that had come out of the ark, and all their descendants. As a sign of the covenant he created the rainbow: whenever a rainbow appeared, it would remind him of the promise he had made to 'every living being, comprising all flesh that is on earth'.[7] To Noah's sons, Shem, Ham and Japheth, he assigned a task: 'Be fertile and increase and fill the earth.'[8] They fulfilled that task: all people on earth are descended from them. And the other creatures too carried out God's intention that they should 'swarm on earth, and breed and increase on it'.[9]

Noah still had a long life ahead of him – he died at the age of 950. But what is told of his life after the Flood – how he became a farmer and invented viticulture, how he got drunk, how his son Ham saw him naked and his other sons avoided doing so, how as a result Ham's descendants were condemned to servitude for ever – none of this need concern us. In fact it is more than likely that originally these things were told of someone other than Noah the hero of the Flood.

2

That the biblical and the Mesopotamian stories are related is evident from the numerous parallels between the two.[10] In both, the Flood forms one episode in a history which starts before the

Within the mosaic:

DIX=
ᵺDOMINS AD NOE ARCV MEV PONAM
IN NVBIB7 7ERIT SIGNV FEDIS:I
7OM̃E:7TRADN̄ ERV TVIT̃AB
DILVVTĨ AD DELENDA̅ VN̄         NOE·
VERSÃ CARNEM:

6   After the Flood. Noah
sacrifices, God responds.
Mosaic, Cathedral of Monreale,
twelfth-century.

creation of mankind. Moreover it is a divinely decreed episode: Enlil and Yahweh alike implement it. The survival of Noah, as of Atrahasis, is due to divine intervention: both are warned by a god of the impending cataclysm. And the parallelism goes much further than that. In Genesis, as in Tablet IX of *Gilgamesh*, the hero receives divine instructions on how to build the ark with storeys and decks and compartments and a roof and a hatch, and to insulate the whole with pitch. In Genesis as in the *Atrahasis Epic* there are a reconnoitring raven and dove, and a sweet-smelling sacrifice accepted and enjoyed.

The connection is clear – and since the Mesopotamian story was written down centuries before the people of Israel came into being, the biblical story must be derived from it. This need not mean that the biblical author(s) drew directly on *Atrahasis* or on *Gilgamesh*: the Mesopotamian story was very popular and was widely disseminated in various versions.

But though the biblical story is, incontestably, modelled on the Mesopotamian, the purport of the two could not be more different. In the Mesopotamian story the catastrophe that is visited upon mankind is wholly disproportionate; it is caused not by any sinfulness of human beings but by the impatience and imprudence of the gods. And these gods are neither omnipotent nor intelligent: their designs can be frustrated in part by one of their own number – and on the occasion when they are carried out, the result plunges the gods first into panic, then into bitter recrimination.

Above all, Yahweh is very different from Enlil. Granted, he is just as merciless, just as determined to exterminate mankind – but his motives are different. Yahweh acts as a judge who is outraged at the infraction of the divinely established law. In the Genesis story the world before the Flood is shown as chaotic – and the responsibility for the all-pervading disorder lies with all living beings, not simply human beings. The very earth has been corrupted by the misconduct of the creatures that live on it. In sending the Flood God aims not only at punishing the guilty but at purifying a polluted earth.

And of course – the biggest difference of all – Yahweh is no mere chief of the gods, he is the one and only god.

### 3

It has long been recognized that the Old Testament (or Hebrew Bible) is the work of men who collected traditional material and edited it. Of the four groups of collectors/redactors who are held to have made contributions, two are thought to have contributed to Genesis 6–9 – the two known as J (from the German for 'Yahwist') and P (for Priestly). The J and P contributions do not constitute separate portions of the Flood narrative but are interwoven. And there are inconsistencies – notably about the number of pairs of animals and birds to be saved, and about the duration of the Flood. However, such differences are of limited importance. J and P alike are deeply indebted to Mesopotamian models, and both are concerned to transform those models. The biblical story as we possess it is a coherent one.

The values that permeate that story are those of P, and they point to a specific historical context.[11] For, whereas the date of

J is still under discussion, we know the date at which P was at work: some time between 550 and 450 BCE. That means that the story of the Flood as we know it was composed either during the Babylonian Exile or under the impact of that experience.

It was a shattering experience. When in 597 BCE the Babylonian monarch Nebuchadnezzar occupied Jerusalem, most of the inhabitants who possessed either influence or skill were deported to Babylon: the king and his family, the palace officials, the well-to-do and the educated, also smiths, metal-workers, craftsmen of all kinds. A few years later the walls of Jerusalem were razed and Solomon's temple burned to the ground. The Davidic monarchy, which had ruled for four centuries, was finally eliminated. The state collapsed, Judah lost the last remnants of political independence.

This disaster was experienced as a collapse of the ordered world itself. As he contemplated the ruins of Jerusalem, the prophet Jeremiah felt that he was witnessing a return to primordial chaos:

> I saw the earth, and it was without form and void;
>     the heavens, and their light was gone.
> I saw the mountains, and they reeled;
>     all the hills rocked to and fro.
> I saw, and there was no man,
>     and the very birds had taken flight.[12]

That is the context in which the biblical story of the Flood should be interpreted. In Ancient Near Eastern literature invasion and conquest are commonly symbolized by storm and flood, sent by divine decree – and so it is here. But there is more to it than that. In the Flood the 'bars and doors' that God had fixed to keep the turbulent waters in place are broken through, with the result that the cosmos dissolves into chaos. The destruction of Judah and Jerusalem and the Temple meant no less.

But in that case the righteous Noah and his family must stand for a minority of Israelites who because of their righteousness have been spared from the catastrophe – the 'remnant' which, as so often in the Hebrew Bible, is saved in order to carry out the divine intention for the world. And since P is writing for the exilic community – whether in Babylon or shortly after the return to Judah – those righteous ones must belong to that community.[13]

But what did it mean, to be righteous? P wrote at a time when Israelite religion was undergoing a transformation.[14] The god Yahweh, who in the past had been simply the patron god of a small people, was coming to be perceived as the one and only true god, creator of the world and all creatures on it, judge of all mankind, omnipotent and omniscient. From that time onwards Israelite – or, as it came to be called, Jewish – righteousness consisted above all in exclusive devotion to the one true god.

This new kind of religion – whether one calls it henotheism or monotheism – flourished first amongst the exiles and continued to flourish amongst those who returned from exile to Judah. By his (or their) very nature, the priestly author(s) belonged amongst its most passionate propagandists: a major part of the Hebrew Bible is there to prove it – and that includes Genesis 6–9. One can hardly imagine a more resounding proclamation of the heightened dignity of Yahweh than his warning to Noah: 'I have decided to put an end to all flesh, for the earth is filled with lawlessness because of them. So I am about to destroy both them and the earth.'

The contrast with the Mesopotamian story could hardly be more absolute. The scribes who composed the *Atrahasis Epic* were concerned to demote the supreme god in the interest of a lesser god with whom they could identify. The priestly authors who shaped the Genesis story were concerned to promote their god to a position of unique dignity. The god who decrees the biblical Flood is indeed enormously impressive. Not to be questioned, not to be reasoned with, not even to be understood, in solitary and terrifying majesty he decides the perdition or salvation of the world and all that is in it.

Throughout the long history of Flood interpretation, down to the present day, the deity who presides over the great cataclysm has continued to be imagined in that way.

4

So that is how the biblical account of the Flood came into

7  George Smith.
Engraving, artist
unknown.

being: a story originally inspired by Mesopotamian experiences
of flood was adapted to reflect the experience and aspirations of
Judaeans exiled in Mesopotamia or recently returned from Mesopotamia. Not an unfamiliar notion nowadays, but it may be worth
noting what a relatively new notion it is. Nobody could have
entertained it before 1872. Until then everybody took for granted
that the Genesis story was the original story; nobody knew, or even
suspected, that it had a Mesopotamian prototype.

The change in perspective was due to a very extraordinary man
with a very ordinary name, George Smith.[15] Born in London in
1840, Smith was put, at the age of fourteen, to learn bank-note
engraving – an occupation for which he showed such talent that
he seemed well set to become one of the master engravers of the
century. But his interest lay elsewhere – in the civilizations of
the Ancient Near East, which he got to know not only through the
Old Testament – especially the Books of Genesis, Samuel
and Kings – but above all through the books in which Austen
Layard described his excavation of the royal palaces of Assyria.

The middle years of the nineteenth century were one of the
most brilliant periods in the history of eastern archaeology. Discovery after discovery was being made, to the astonishment of the

world; and in 1857 the cryptograph of cuneiform writings was being unravelled. George Smith was enthralled. His meagre savings went into the purchase of books on cuneiform and its decipherment, his evenings were spent in studying them.

The boy spent so much of his holidays and dinner-times in the British Museum, amongst the newly acquired treasures from Nineveh and Babylon, that he came to the notice of the Keeper of Oriental Antiquities. Soon he had given up bank-note engraving and started work at the Museum as a 'repairer', charged with the task of examining and sorting thousands of inscribed fragments of cuneiform and joining together those which belonged to the same original tablet. He showed himself a genius at reading texts; when faced with words that he did not know, he still divined what an inscription must mean – and he was almost always right. Soon he began to publish the results of his work. His classic *History of Ashurbanipal* is a monument to his mastery of cuneiform. His labours in that field did not prevent him from deciphering the values of Cypriote characters from a bilingual text of Cypriote and Phoenician. No wonder that in 1866 he was appointed Assistant in the Department of Oriental Antiquities.

Smith's zeal was boundless. He worked ceaselessly, and was furious when the London fogs, and the almost total lack of artificial lighting in the Museum, interrupted his labours. The copies of Assyrian tablets which he prepared for lithographing were of an extraordinary quality, given the imperfect state of Assyriological knowledge: nobody else at that time could have done as well.

It was while sorting and classifying fragments of tablets from Ashurbanipal's famous library at Nineveh that Smith stumbled upon the discovery that was to make him famous. Many of the fragments, he observed, contained bits of mythical stories – and one large fragment seemed to tell of a flood. He has told, as modestly as may be, what happened then:

> . . . my eye caught the statement that the ship rested on the mountains of Nizir, followed by the account of the sending forth of the dove, and its finding no resting-place and returning. I saw at once that I had here discovered a portion at least of the Chaldaean account of the Deluge.

Smith had hit upon the eleventh of the twelve chapters which make up *Gilgamesh* – and, by a happy chance, it was one of the best preserved of all. As more fragments turned up, it became possible to complete most of the story as it originally was. On 3 December 1872, Smith read a paper on this astonishing find to the Society of Biblical Archaeology; those present on the platform included the Prime Minister, Gladstone, the Dean of Westminster, Arthur Stanley, and a number of distinguished scholars, theologians and archaeologists. Smith's discovery made a profound impression on his hearers, and the news soon spread abroad. Such was the popular enthusiasm that the *Daily Telegraph* offered the (at that time very substantial) sum of 1,000 guineas to enable Smith to make fresh excavations in Ashurbanipal's library at Nineveh, in the hope of finding more fragments of the same tablet.

With no training or previous experience as a field archaeologist, and with the temperament of a scholar rather than an organizer, Smith undertook the task – and within a week of starting excavation had found and deciphered a fragment (now known to belong to *Atrahasis*) which filled the only important gap in the story of the Flood. Two further expeditions, in 1874 and 1875–6, were subsidized by the Trustees of the British Museum, and on the second of these Smith caught dysentery and died, at the age of thirty-six. In all he had collected some three thousand fragments of tablets, which are now in the British Museum. He had also transformed all ideas about where and when our western story of the Flood took shape.

8  Noah's emergence from the ark, prefiguring Christ's resurrection. Fresco from the catacombs of Saints Peter and Marcellinus, Rome, fourth-century.

# Chapter 3
## *Hidden Meanings*

1

Early Christian writers took it for granted that the events recounted in the Old Testament had really happened. However, their main concern was to find, in those long past happenings, prefigurings of the present and the future.

This kind of exegesis is known as typology; it is based on the conviction that nothing in the Old Testament can be understood aright save in terms of the Christian revelation. A modern scholar has described this approach as 'the unhistorical attitude which saw in the Bible a vast harmonious complex of prophecy and fulfilment, type and antitype, allegorical picture and spiritual reality, fused together by the uniform inspiration of the Holy Spirit'. To illustrate the point he quotes Augustine: 'In the Old Testament the New lies hid; in the New Testament the meaning of the Old becomes clear.'[1] Many a Christian theologian could be quoted to the same effect, and ordinary Bible readers held to this assumption right up to the late nineteenth century.

Typology was applied to the story of the Flood.[2] Already the Jewish apocalypse *1 Enoch*, which was well known and highly esteemed in the early Christian communities, had presented the Flood as in a sense prefiguring the End of Time. Many early Christians lived in tense expectation of the return of Christ to judge the world; and by them too the Flood was perceived as prefiguring the flood of fire that would follow then. As the Gospel of Matthew puts it:

As were the days of Noah, so will be the coming of the Son of man. For as in those days before the flood they were eating and drinking, marrying and giving in marriage, until the day when Noah entered the ark, and they did not know until the flood came and swept them all away, so will be the coming of the Son of man.[3]

The Second Letter of Peter is even more explicit:

. . . by the word of God . . . the world that then existed was deluged with water and perished. But by the same word the heavens and earth that now exist have been stored up for fire, being kept until the day of judgment and the destruction of ungodly men.[4]

The figure of Noah was reinterpreted accordingly: he came to symbolize the believing Christians who, because they lived with the Last Judgment always in mind, would be singled out to be saved when it came. To illustrate the precept that 'faith is the assurance of things hoped for, the conviction of things not seen' the Letter to the Hebrews comments, 'By faith Noah, being warned by God concerning events as yet unseen, took heed and constructed an ark for the saving of his household.'[5] The notion of Noah as an exemplar of righteousness, in the sense of unquestioning obedience to God, became commonplace; and soon it was carried further. Noah came to be seen as a sort of John the Baptist, warning of the imminent judgment.

Although there is not a word in Genesis to suggest that Noah preached, he was cast as a preacher of righteousness. Here too a New Testament text supplied the necessary authority: in the Second Letter of Peter, Noah is referred to as 'a herald of righteousness' in the days of the flood. Clement of Rome, writing in the last years of the first century, is more specific: Noah preached repentance, and those who took heed were saved.[6] And Theophilus, Bishop of Antioch in the late second century, states that Noah warned his contemporaries that the Flood was coming and urged them to repent.[7] Other writers of the second and third centuries went much further still: God bade Noah make a rattle to attract the attention of the inattentive, and he did so; and he preached again and again, he even preached for a hundred years

9  Noah as a 'type' of Christ; a theme which flourished throughout the middle ages. Fresco from St Savin-sur-Gartempe, near Poitiers, twelfth-century.

on end – but in vain. Nobody would listen, for all were given over to sin, to murder and wars, adultery and intemperance, and every kind of vice.[8]

So, it is implied, God delayed the Flood – and this too was a prefiguring. Here too the Second Letter of Peter is instructive. Writing after 100 CE, perhaps as late as 140, the author felt it necessary to explain why Christ had not returned: God did not wish that any should perish, but that all should have time to repent before the earth and everything on it was burned up.[9] Justin, in the mid-second century, brought this notion into relation with the Flood. The fire of judgment, he declared, would dissolve all things just as the waters of the Flood left none alive save Noah and his family. And as the Flood was delayed to enable Noah to complete his preaching, so the fiery catastrophe was being delayed to enable people to repent.[10]

The glorification of Noah did not stop there: in some quarters he came to be seen as the 'type' of Christ. His survival and his emergence from the ark were interpreted as prefiguring the resurrection of Christ and his emergence from the tomb – and so the resurrection to eternal life which is the hope of every Christian. Some pushed the parallelism even further – for was not Noah, like Christ, the chief of a new, regenerated race? To Origen he was the

founder of a new universe, the progenitor of the new, post-
diluvian mankind.[11] Noah was also called 'the end of the forego-
ing generations and the beginning of those that were to come': a
kind of second root of the human race.[12] The very name Noah was
believed (wrongly) to be a Hebrew word meaning 'rest' – and this
in itself seemed to point forward to the Christ who said 'Come to
me . . . and I will give you rest.'[13] Cyril of Jerusalem even speaks of
Christ as 'the true Noah', while Ephraem Syrus tells how the hero
of the Flood, although giving what rest he could, longed to see the
one of whom he was the 'type' and who would give it more amply.
Similar associations are to be found in Cyril of Alexandria and in
Augustine.[14]


2


One form of typology is allegory. For a master of allegorical
interpretation every episode or utterance in the Old Testament,
however obscure, contained some allusion to the facts narrated in
the gospels. It was his task to discern those hidden allusions and to
reveal their true meanings. And the meanings could be multiple:
the typologist felt free to attach to each episode as many meanings
as he chose – never doubting that all those meanings had been
intended by God when he arranged for the episode to be
recorded.

The allegorical method could produce strange results. For
Justin, the whole mystery of salvation through Christ is prefigured
in the story of the Flood. The wood of the ark prefigured the
cross. That eight persons had been saved in the ark (Noah and his
wife, and their three sons and their wives) prefigured the resurrection of Christ, which took place on the day after the Sabbath –
which in the earliest liturgies was treated as the eighth day of the
week as well as the first. The fact that the Flood covered the whole
earth indicated that God's message was intended for all mankind
and not merely for Jews.[15]

Such extravagances were not confined to relatively minor
figures like Justin. Irenaeus, Bishop of Lyons towards the end
of the second century, is commonly regarded as the first major
Christian theologian – and when he came to reflect on the

10   Noah emerging from the ark. Another interpretation of
Noah as 'type' of Christ. From the catacombs of Saints Peter
and Marcellinus.

parallelism between the Flood and the Last Judgment he was happy to link the number of the beast in Revelation 13, 666, with Noah's age at the time of the Flood, 600, plus the height of the golden statue in the Book of Daniel, sixty cubits, plus its breadth, six cubits.[16] The greatest and most enduringly influential of the Greek Fathers, Origen, noted that the animals in the ark were assigned to different rooms, and commented that this symbolized the various degrees of spiritual progress attained by members of the Church.[17]

The greatest and most enduringly influential of the Latin Fathers, Augustine, was even more ingenious. In *The City of God* he writes as follows:

> Undoubtedly, the ark is a symbol of the City of God on its pilgrimage in history, a figure of the Church which was saved by the wood on which there hung the 'Mediator between God and men, himself man, Christ Jesus'. Even the very measurements of length, height, and breadth of the ark are meant to point to the reality of the human body into which he came as it was foretold that he would come. It will be recalled that the length of a normal body from head to foot is six times the breadth from one side to the other and ten times the thickness from back to front. Measure a man who is lying prone on the ground. He is six times as long from head to foot as he is wide from side to side, and he is ten times as long as he is high from the ground up. That is why the ark was made 300 cubits in length, fifty in breadth, and thirty in height. As for the door in the side, that, surely, symbolizes the open wound made by the lance in the side of the Crucified – the door by which those who come to him enter in, in the sense that believers enter the Church by means of the sacraments which issued from that wound. It was ordered that the ark should be made out of squared timbers – a symbol of the four-square stability of a holy life, which, like a cube, stands firm however it is turned. So it is with every other detail of the ark's construction. They are all symbols of something in the Church.
> . . .
> Any interpretation which is to catch the mind of the writer who described the Flood must realize the connections of this story with the City of God which, in this wicked world, is ever tossed like the ark in the waters of a deluge. . . . I said, for

instance, that the words, 'with lower, middle chambers, and third storeys shall they make it', can be applied to the Church. The Church is gathered from all nations, and is two-storeyed because it has room for two kinds of men, the circumcised and the uncircumcised . . . But the Church is also three-storeyed because after the Flood the whole world was repeopled with descendants from the three sons of Noah.

Now, anyone is entitled to say something else, so long as what he says is in harmony with the rule of faith. Thus, God wanted the ark to have rooms not only in the lower storey but also in the middle storey – the 'middle chambers' – and even in the top storey – the 'third storey' – so that there should be living space from the bottom to the top. These storeys may well be taken to imply the three virtues praised by the Apostle: faith, hope and charity. However, better application would be to the three harvest-increases mentioned in the Gospel, the thirty-fold, sixty-fold and hundred-fold, the meaning being that on the lowest level in the Church we have chaste marriage, on the next level chaste widowhood, and on the highest level virginal purity.[18]

Augustine was writing some four centuries after the time of Jesus, and the Last Judgment had not come. Salvation and damnation were no longer imagined in the setting of an imminent End. The world remained, and with the world, the Church, as the perennial mediator of salvation. The story of the Flood was reinterpreted accordingly. The ark by which God had saved a remnant of mankind symbolized the Church by which God was saving Christians. That there was only one ark demonstrated that there was only one valid Church. All outside it were doomed to perish: 'This is the ark of Noah, and he who is not in it shall perish when the Flood prevails,' wrote Jerome of the Church; and Augustine used the same image in his catechetical teaching.[19] Some went further. It is characteristic of typological doctrine that present reality surpasses the 'type' that prefigures it. Thus a fourth-century Archbishop of Constantinople, John Chrysostom, could insist:

Just as in the midst of the sea the ark saved those who were inside it, so the Church saves all who have strayed. But whereas the ark merely saved, the Church does more than that. For instance, the ark received animals deprived of reason, and saved them, but still deprived of reason; whereas the Church receives human beings deprived of reason but does not keep them like that, it transforms them.[20]

The equation of ark and Church has maintained itself down the centuries. It is still there in the Anglican rite of baptism:

> Almighty and everlasting God, who of thy great mercy didst save Noah and his family in the ark from perishing by water . . . We beseech thee, by thine infinite mercies, that thou wilt mercifully look upon this child . . . that he, being delivered from thy wrath, may be received into the ark of Christ's Church; and being steadfast in faith, joyful through hope, and rooted in charity, may so pass through the waves of this troublesome world, that finally he may come to the land of everlasting life . . .

The Flood itself continued to provoke much thought. Occasionally, a phrase in the Book of Revelation (17: 15) – 'The waters that you saw . . . are peoples and multitudes and nations and tongues' – was interpreted as meaning that the Flood prefigured the persecution of the Church by the heathen. But the interpretation that established itself was a less obvious one: no longer perceived as a hostile, destructive force, the Flood became a 'type' of the saving rite of baptism.

No theme recurs more frequently in the writings of the Fathers. Again and again the world emerging purified from the Flood is compared with the convert emerging purified of sin from the baptismal waters. Cyprian makes the comparison explicit: he refers to the Flood as 'that baptism of the world'.[21] Ambrose, Bishop of Milan in the fourth century, is eloquent on the subject:

> You see the water, you see the wood, you behold the dove, yet you have doubts about the mystery? It is the water in which the flesh is dipped to wash away all carnal sin.[22]

Just as, in the Genesis story, 'all flesh' was destroyed by the Flood, so 'the outer man' is destroyed by baptism. And for Augustine the fact that the Flood rose high above the mountains signifies that the sacrament of baptism rises high above the wisdom of the proud.[23] The ark which saves from the Flood as prefiguring the Church, the Flood itself as prefiguring the saving rite of baptism – paradoxical though it may seem, both notions became commonplaces.

No feature of the biblical story escaped typological interpretation. For Jerome, the raven which Noah sent forth from the ark, and which did not return, was 'the foul bird of wickedness' which is expelled by baptism.[24] Augustine detected in the unfortunate bird a 'type' of impure men who crave for things outside the Church.[25]

More important was the dove: clearly it prefigured that other dove which, embodying the Holy Spirit, descended on Jesus at his baptism. The olive branch which the dove brought back to Noah of course symbolized peace. The return of the dove with the olive branch was a favourite theme for early Christian art: on sarcophagi and in the catacombs it epitomized the hope of resurrection and life everlasting.[26] The dove's return to the ark could also symbolize man's need to belong to the Church, the impossibility of living outside it. However, others believed that it symbolized the rejection of Jesus by the Jews. Like the dove when it was taken back into the ark, Jesus (so to speak) found a resting place among the Gentiles when they received the gospel.[27]

Typological and allegorical speculations had great fascination, and they persisted right down to the late seventeenth century. But Genesis 6–9 lent itself also to other kinds of imaginative elaboration, which have lasted even longer.

# Chapter 4

## *Filling Gaps*

1

What could be more enthralling than to treat the story of the Flood as a realistic but incomplete historical narrative – to enquire after all those points of detail which Genesis failed to consider, to solve all those problems which it failed to tackle? Jews as well as Christians addressed these tasks with enthusiasm. What the rabbis made of the matter can be gathered, for instance, from the Midrash *Genesis Rabbah.*[1] The work follows Genesis verse by verse; and although the rabbinic sayings it records date from various times up to the fifth century, and sometimes diverge widely, an overall picture emerges clearly enough.

The time before the Flood, we are told, was a time of prosperity and ease. It was a perpetual springtime; there were no dangerous animals; grain needed to be sown only once in forty years.[2] Women bore children after a single day of pregnancy, and children could walk and talk from the moment of their birth. Unfortunately people showed no gratitude for these blessings – indeed, they went so far as to say, 'What is the Almighty that we should serve him?'[3] But what most offended God was their unchastity, for 'God is patient with all sins save only an immoral life'. And licentiousness was indeed boundless: men were masturbating on trees and stones, they were fornicating with other men's wives, with their own daughters, with other men, with animals; they would take two wives and make one sterile so as to enjoy her without risk of procreation. Nuptial songs were composed in honour of sodomy and bestiality.[4] No wonder that the disorder extended to all species: just as man mated with beasts, so the dog mated with the wolf, the cock with the peahen.[5] Some rabbis asserted that God's decision to destroy 'all flesh', animals along with human beings, was a natural response to this universal corruption. (It is true that another view was maintained with equal conviction: that the animals were destroyed because, with mankind gone, they were no longer of any use.)

Then there were the robberies that people committed. If a farmer brought a basket of vegetables to market, each thief would steal a tiny amount, so as not to be liable to a criminal charge; but before long the farmer would have nothing left to sell.[6] From the rising to the setting of the sun there was no good in human beings – and they were no better at night.[7] Even when Noah warned of the impending Flood – and he did so for 120 years – people were unmoved. After all, they argued, if the water really came up from the depths they could always cover the earth with iron plates; and if it came from above, they knew a remedy for that too. And so far from repenting, people became ever more wicked.

Noah of course was an exception – but even he was righteous only in comparison with the wicked of his generation; compared with Moses or even Samuel, he would not have been righteous.[8] Noah, some rabbis held, lacked faith; it was only when the water reached his ankles that he entered the ark. Others went so far as to say that Noah possessed less than an ounce of merit; if God saved him nevertheless, that was simply because Moses was fated to descend from him.[9] That was one view of the matter. There was another, contrary view. It could be argued that if Noah managed to stay righteous in such a deplorable generation, he would have done even better if he had lived in the time of Moses. Even as it was, he was a comfort to himself, to his forefathers, and to the world.[10]

There was no more agreement about the plan of the ark. One rabbi held that the ark had 330 compartments, each ten cubits square, arranged in four rows, separated by two corridors four cubits wide; and there was a gangway around the outside, of a cubit's width. The ark tapered inwards: the upper storey had only three rows of compartments. But another rabbi insisted that there

11    Panic as the Flood starts. A painting by Jan van Scorel (1495–1562).

were no less than 900 compartments, each six cubits square, arranged in six rows, with three corridors of four cubits' width, and with a gangway of two cubits' width on the outside. This ark had straight sides, but a sloping roof of a cubit's height. As for the location of the garbage – top floor or bottom? – that too was a matter of dispute. And likewise the accommodation of the unclean animals: top floor or bottom? All these divergent views were maintained by one rabbi or another.[11]

The nature of the food eaten in the ark was also a matter of debate. There were those who held that only dried figs were eaten; but other rabbis insisted that suitable food for each species was taken aboard – branches for the elephants, glass for the ostriches, and so on.[12] Also, shoots of vine, fig and olive must have been taken, for future planting. As for the animals, only those were admitted which had avoided sin by mating always with their own kind – but was that enough? Not everyone thought so. Some held that species where the male pursued the female were acceptable, but not those where the female pursued the male.[13] Fish, it was generally thought, were immune from drowning; nevertheless, it could be argued that they too would have been gathered into the ark if they had not all fled to the Mediterranean. There was much argument about the *re'em*, an unusually large animal of uncertain identity. Was it tied to the outside of the ark? Or was only its head accommodated inside the ark? Or maybe only its whelps were admitted? Each opinion had its exponents.[14]

During the seven days between the closing of the ark and the onset of the Flood the wild beasts that were not taken in stayed around the ark. So did the 700,000 human beings who had remained impenitent. When the Flood began, these people tried to take the ark by storm; but the wild beasts set on them and killed many of them.[15] An even worse fate befell the rest. The waters of the Flood were boiling hot, for only so could the inflamed sensuality of the sinners be appropriately punished; the generation of the Flood was tormented like the people of Sodom, who were consumed by fire.[16]

Even inside the ark life was difficult. There was general agreement amongst the rabbis that sexual intercourse was forbidden; the raven, dog and Noah's son Ham were all punished for failing to observe this prohibition[17] (Ham's punishment was that his descendants would be black). The animals' needs threw a heavy burden on Noah and his family. They had to be fed at the times when they normally ate, day or night. The chameleon presented a special problem: nobody knew what to feed it. Fortunately, Noah let a worm drop from a pomegranate, and the chameleon ate it, after which Noah grew worms for the fastidious creature. The phoenix offered to do without food, to save Noah trouble; the patriarch responded by promising that it would never die. Even so, Noah was kept so busy for twelve months that he never got a wink of sleep.[18]

The raven caused Noah much embarrassment. When the ark came to rest on Ararat, and Noah got ready to send the raven out, the cantankerous bird argued back. Noah, he said, must hate him; for if he suffered a mishap, there would be no more ravens. Also,

12 *Right*: The dove and the raven, devouring a carcass. From the Basel *Speculum*, 1476.

13 *Facing page*: After the Flood. From Kircher's *Arca Noë*, 1675.

he suspected that Noah had designs on his mate, the female raven.[19] Noah tried to reassure him by pointing out that he had been able to stay chaste throughout the time in the ark – but according to one famous rabbi the raven was unconvinced: it remained so anxious on its mate's behalf that it refused to fly off and continued to circle the ark. Mercifully, the dove was more obliging – but that too had its problematic side: where did it find that olive twig? Some rabbis held that the twig came from the flowering shrubs of the land of Israel, others from the Mount of Olives, others again from the Garden of Eden.[20] It was a real problem, for the earth's surface was totally devastated: the very furrows left by the plough were washed away. In fact the world was brought back to its primeval state, before the creation of man.

After the disembarkation on Ararat a sacrifice was offered to God – but was it offered by Noah? There was a theory that Noah, having once forgotten to give the lion its daily ration, was attacked and lamed by the enraged beast and no longer possessed the bodily wholeness that a priest had to have. So, who put on the

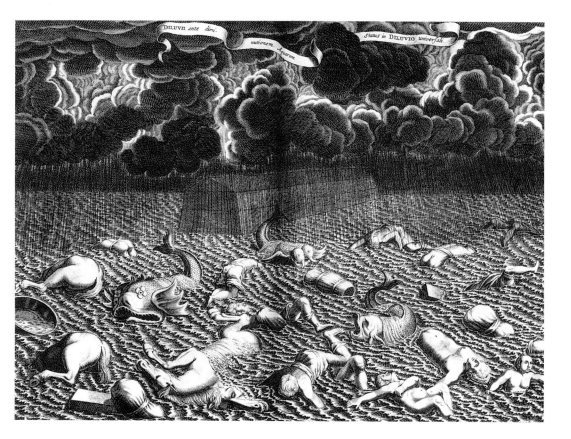

priestly garments which had been bestowed on Adam and had been handed down to the first-born in each generation? If some were convinced that the happy man was indeed Noah, others held that it was Noah's son Shem.[21] In any event, God was pleased with the sacrifice, and promised that he would not again curse the earth: the curse uttered in the days of Adam would suffice. And if in future human beings became intolerably wicked again, only the wicked part of mankind would be annihilated.

## 2

The speculations outlined above arose very easily from the Haggadic method of scriptural exegesis, which is a peculiarly Jewish method. However, very similar speculations also flourished amongst Christians. Indeed, amongst Christians they continued to proliferate right down to the seventeenth century, as a tradition parallel to the typological/allegorical tradition, and no less vigorous.[22]

Already Origen, in the third century, was provoked by one Apelles – a disciple of the celebrated Gnostic Marcion – who declared that the ark described in Genesis would hardly be large enough to house four elephants. Genesis, like the rest of the Pentateuch, was of course believed to have been written by Moses; so Origen could counter that argument by pointing out that Moses grew up in Egypt, where 'cubit' meant the geometrical cubit, which is six times larger than the common cubit.

As described by Origen, the ark was a truncated pyramid, measuring 300 cubits by fifty at the base and only one cubit by one at the apex. It had five decks: the upper three for the human beings, for clean animals, and for carnivores and reptiles respectively; the lower two for food and offal.[23] Later writers produced variations: the ark had four floors occupied, in descending order, by the Noah family, domestic animals, reptiles, and wild animals:[24] or it had three floors, for the Noah family surrounded by birds, for clean animals, and for unclean animals.[25] But the ark remained pyramidal in shape until the twelfth century, when it came to be thought of as a rectangular house with a sloping roof.

However, it was in the late middle ages that the realistic approach really came into its own. By the fifteenth century one Alfonso Tostado felt able to give a detailed account of life inside the ark:

And because Noah took care of the animals and gave them food which was kept in the apotheca on the second level, there was a stairway from the habitation of Noah to this place so that he could descend and take up food. So he gave them food, walking between the apes, dragons, unicorns, and elephants, who thanks to God did not harm him but waited for him to give them nourishment at the proper time. The divine pleasure saw to it that there was a great peace among these animals; the lion did not hurt the unicorn, or the dragon the elephants, or the falcon the dove. There was also a vent in the habitation of the tame animals and another in that of the wild animals through which dung was conveyed to the sentina. Noah and his sons collected the dung and cast it by means of an orifice into the sentina so that the animals would not rot in their own offal. One could also believe that the odour of the dung was miraculously carried off so that the air was not corrupted and men and

ARCA NOE

14   The ark and its occupants. From the *Silos Apocalypse*, 1109.

15    Inside the ark. From Kircher's *Arca Noë*, 1675.

animals were not slain by the pest. So the men in the ark laboured daily and had no great time for leisure.[26]

It remained for the great geometrician Johannes Buteo in the mid-sixteenth century to calculate the precise dimensions of the ark.[27] Using the common cubit, he arrived at 457,500 cubic cubits for the interior area of the ark. After subtracting the space occupied by stairways, partitions, beams and joists, there was left a usable space of 350,000 cubic cubits. Buteo estimated that the larger animals would need the same space as ninety-one cows, the smaller animals would require the same space as eighty sheep, the carnivores the same space as eighty wolves. He further estimated that a deck would take 300 stalls – with the happy result that all the animals could be accommodated in a quarter of the ark's area. The 146,000 cubic cubits of hay that would be required to feed the ruminants for a year would fit nicely into the 150,000 cubic cubits of the second deck. That would leave room on the top deck for Noah's grinding mills and ovens (with smokeless fuel) for baking and cooking. There would even be room for an aquarium – though Buteo was uncertain whether that would be necessary, as fish might well be without sin and would therefore be spared.

Buteo's version of the ark was adopted as a model by many

other commentators – even if they modified it, for instance, to provide sheep for the carnivores to eat. Most agreed that the snakes would have made no difficulty, as they could wind themselves round the beams and rafters. They also agreed that hybrids must have been excluded, as they were unable to reproduce: not only the mule but the tragelaph (deer and goat), the allopecopithicum (wolf and ape), the armadillo (hedgehog and tortoise), and the marmota (badger and squirrel) were condemned species. That all the inmates of the ark had to be sexually continent for the duration was taken for granted.

Nevertheless, some vexatious problems remained. God had commanded that the creatures should be admitted in pairs – so what of the phoenix, which is male and female in itself? Or the vulture, which is always female in gender and is fecundated by the wind? Again, it was certain that the bird of paradise had no feet, so had to fly all the time: did it fly in the ark, or in the air above the ark? Sirens, too, were a problem: they certainly existed – one commentator actually possessed the skeleton of a siren – so they must have survived the Flood; but did that mean that they were admitted to the ark, or were they, like other amphibians, quartered safely on its outside? There was no consensus on any of these matters.

By the seventeenth century the matter of strange species and their survival was becoming still more perplexing. Explorers of South America frequently brought back animals of kinds that were quite unknown in the Old World. How had they got there in the first place? In the 1620s Robert Burton posed the question in *The Anatomy of Melancholy*:

> Why so many thousand strange birds and beasts proper to *America* alone, as Acosta demands . . . Were they created in six days, or ever in *Noah's* ark? If there, why were they not dispersed & found in other countries? It is a thing (saith he) hath long held me in suspense; no *Greek, Latin, Hebrew* ever heard of them before, and yet as differing from our European animals, as an egg and a chestnut . . .[28]

Of course, human beings had migrated all over the globe after the Flood – Genesis said so – and no doubt they took many

16  The ark with sirens alongside. From the Quentell Bible, Cologne, *c.* 1478.

animals with them; but that did not explain those hitherto unknown species. Nor did it explain the presence in America of noxious creatures which ought to have vanished for ever in the Flood. Who, for instance, would have gone to the trouble of transporting rattlesnakes? The Norwich physician Sir Thomas Browne, in his *Pseudodoxia Epidemica* (1646), admitted his perplexity:

> How America abounded with Beasts of prey and noxious Animals, yet contained not in it that necessary Creature, a Horse, is very strange. By what passage those, not only Birds, but dangerous and unwelcome Beasts, came over; how there be Creatures there which are not found in this Triple Continent; all of which must needs be strange unto us, that hold but one Ark, and that the Creatures began their progress from the Mountains of Ararat . . .[29]

Neither Burton nor Browne suggested any solution; but some did begin to wonder whether perhaps the Flood had been less universal than was commonly believed.

3

There were other reasons for doubting whether the Flood could have been truly universal. The growth of scientific curiosity in the course of the seventeenth century led some intellectuals to wonder where such a vast quantity of water could have come from, and where it could have gone after the Flood was over.[30] For Catholic theologians this was no great problem: for them the Flood was a miracle, for which a rational explanation was neither possible nor desirable. Protestants, on the other hand, were concerned to show that Scripture and reason were at one, here as elsewhere. And a few audacious spirits went so far as to argue that the Flood must have been only a local catastrophe.

In 1655 a French Calvinist, Isaac La Peyrère, published in Amsterdam a small volume entitled *Prae-Adamitae*, in which he maintained that God had created multitudes of human beings before he created Adam, who was simply the first Jew. Nor did God intend to destroy all mankind in the Flood – he was concerned only with his chosen people, the Jews, who had offended him by interbreeding with Gentiles. The Flood was accordingly limited to Palestine – and as for the land which was divided amongst Noah's sons, that too was limited to Palestine.[31]

This interpretation of the Flood was of course quite unacceptable – as indeed was the whole argument of the *Prae-Adamitae*. The book was attacked and abused in countless books and pamphlets, and the man himself was so persecuted that he ended by renouncing his theory. However, the notion of a local flood soon found less radical advocates. In 1659 the Dutchman Isaak Vossius (Voss) argued that at the time of the Flood most of the earth was still uninhabited: only Mesopotamia and Syria had been populated by the nine generations since Adam, so a flood sent by God to punish mankind could stop there. Nor was Vossius alone. Within a few years the German Georg Kirchmaier was pointing out that the ancients often spoke in universal terms when describing a local event; though the Flood as portrayed in Genesis looks like a universal disaster, in reality it affected only that part of the world where Noah lived. In fact the Bible itself, if one read it attentively, showed how small the area of human habitation was until the dispersion at Babel.[32]

This was a notably rational view – indeed, it was probably as far as anyone could go, while accepting the divine inspiration of the biblical story, towards an understanding of how that story really had originated. However, it was open to an obvious objection. Why, it was asked, if the Flood was merely local, did God bid Noah build an ark, instead of telling him to move, with his family and some animals, to a nearby mountainous terrain?

The traditional view was not to be so easily discredited. Moreover, with the help of a verse of Genesis it too could be made to look quite rational: 'And God made the firmament and separated the waters which were under the firmament from the waters which were above the firmament.'[33] This was commonly taken to mean that there was one mass of water high above the earth, if not above the heavens; and another, even more important mass in a subterranean abyss. As nobody at that time had an inkling of what really lies beneath the earth's crust, this was a plausible supposition. Moreover, observation seemed to confirm the existence of such an abyss. There were enclosed seas, such as the Caspian, into which large rivers flowed, yet which grew no larger: surely, then, they must drain into the abyss? As the extent of evaporation was not appreciated, this explanation seemed reasonable enough.

Already at the beginning of the seventeenth century Sir Walter Raleigh, reflecting on the Flood during his imprisonment in the Tower of London, found an explanation in that same abyss. When the vast quantities of water at the centre of the earth were brought to the surface, he argued, they could provide a belt thirty miles high around the earth. (No smaller amount would serve, for some mountains were thirty miles high.)[34]

In the 1660s, belief in the existence of a watery abyss was powerfully reinforced by the *Mundus Subterraneus* of Athanasius Kircher. The German Jesuit Kircher was both an extraordinarily learned and an extraordinarily adventurous man. Deeply impressed by the great Calabrian earthquake of 1636, he spent many years trying to discover, by travel and observation as well as by study, the causes of earthquakes and volcanic eruptions. He had himself lowered into the craters of Etna and Vesuvius, he investigated deep grottoes and caverns – and he wrote down his observations and illustrated them with charts and diagrams, which were then turned into beautiful plates. On his travels in the

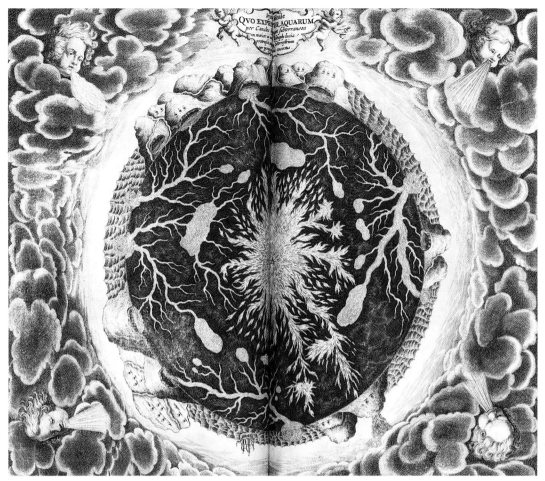

17  Kircher's view of the fire at the earth's centre and the surrounding waters. From the *Mundus Subterraneus*, 1678.

Alps he came across underground streams – waters which must surely have been flowing without cessation since the beginning of the world. Here, he decided, lay some hidden secret of nature – and he was sure, too, that he knew what that secret was: God decreed at the time of the creation of the world that *hydrophylacia* should be formed – giant reservoirs in and under the mountains, all connected with the watery abyss below and with the rivers above.[35] The plates in the *Mundus Subterraneus* show how the water in these *hydropyhlacia* was propelled upwards by fires burning eternally at the centre of the earth, to emerge as rivers and springs.

Kircher's *Arca Noë* of 1675 is wholly devoted to the Flood. There Kircher maintains that when God decided to punish the world through the Flood, he did so by loosing the bonds that held back the waters of the abyss and of the *hydrophylacia*, so that they would rush through the holes and cracks in the earth's surface and overflow everything. And he insists on the supernatural, miraculous character of that happening: by themselves the forces of nature could never have achieved it; only the right hand of the omnipotent Creator of nature was capable of it, and the means by which it was done were beyond human imagining.[36]

Kircher's books were extremely influential, and they certainly stimulated the imagination of certain English thinkers who, in the last two decades of the seventeenth century, formulated new and singularly adventurous interpretations of the Flood. Only, those thinkers were convinced that the means by which God had operated were not really beyond human imagining.

# Chapter 5
## *A Ruined Earth*

1

In the second half of the seventeenth century the Christian religion was gradually ceasing to be what it had been for a thousand years: the core of western culture. Economic activity was ever less effectively restrained by Christian ethics, states were asserting ever more emphatically their supremacy over any church. Above all, science was becoming an autonomous activity, with its own criteria of truth. A new conception of nature as a machine, governed by impersonal laws, was spreading abroad – and was soon to find a glorious confirmation in the achievements of Isaac Newton. This mechanical conception was the first attempt since antiquity at a scientific theory explaining the whole of creation, and it brought new problems. It made it difficult to believe in miracles. Could belief in divine providence itself survive?

It not only survived, it flourished. The tension between religious faith and natural science was not yet experienced as downright conflict, as it would be a century later. Almost every scientist, indeed almost every intellectual with scientific interests, was convinced that science could and must be reconciled with religion. In practice this meant that Christian beliefs were modified to harmonize with the findings of science.

It was in Protestant England that this process was carried furthest. English scientists were not only profoundly, unquestioningly Christian – they were convinced that in studying nature they were studying the unfolding of God's wise and benevolent plan.[1] And this aspiration was nowhere more marked than at Cambridge University. It was Cambridge that produced most of the so-called Latitudinarians – active members of the Church of England who, while deeply religious, were convinced that rational argumentation rather than blind faith was the final arbiter in true Christianity.[2]

It was in this spirit that, between 1681 and 1696, two clerics, both of them Cambridge men, produced works dealing both with Noah's Flood and with the fiery flood at the end of the world. They were Thomas Burnet, a former Fellow of Christ's College; and William Whiston, a former Fellow of Clare Hall, and destined to succeed Newton as Lucasian Professor of Mathematics.[3]

Although they differed on important points, the two agreed on the most important points of all. They both took it for granted that the Flood had been sent by God to punish an incorrigibly wicked mankind. On the strength of that famous passage in the Second Letter of Peter,[4] they both expected another, fiery flood – a cataclysm in which the present world would go under, to be replaced by a very different world. Yet – and there lay their originality – they were also both convinced that God operated always through natural processes, so that the ancient Flood and the final conflagration alike could be explained in scientific terms.

Thomas Burnet (?1636–1715) started his university career at Clare Hall, where he came under the influence of the leading Latitudinarian John Tillotson, later Archbishop of Canterbury, and still more of the Platonist Ralph Cudworth, whom he followed to Christ's when Cudworth became Master of that college. At Christ's Burnet found a new and most stimulating mentor in another Platonist, Henry More, whose approach to biblical exegesis he adopted. Like almost everyone in the seventeenth century (and long after, for that matter) More took it for granted that Genesis had been written by Moses. However, in his *Conjectura Cabbalistica*, published in 1653, he argued that while Moses intended Genesis to be taken literally by simple folk, he expected an elite to read between the lines. When he came to write his own works Burnet would make the same assumption about Genesis.

For some sixteen years Burnet lived among the Cambridge Platonists and absorbed their ideas: he too came to see the existing world as a shadow of a first, lost perfection. Then, in 1671, he set off on the Grand Tour with the Earl of Wiltshire, later Duke of Bolton. He has left an account of the experience that was to determine his future:

> There is nothing doth more awaken our thoughts, or excite our minds to enquire into the causes of such things, than the actual View of them; as I have had experience my self, when it was my Fortune to cross the *Alps* and *Apennine* Mountains; for the Sight of those wild, vast, indigested heaps of Stones and Earth did so deeply stir my fancy, that I was not easy till I could give my self some tolerable account how that confusion came in Nature.[5]

Out of that experience came Burnet's masterpiece, now generally known as *The Sacred Theory of the Earth*. The first version of the book was in Latin and was entitled *Telluris Theoria Sacra*; it was published in 1681 in a limited edition of twenty-five copies. A fuller and more popular version, in English, appeared in 1684, under the title *The Theory of the Earth*; it was dedicated to Charles II. In 1689 came a new edition of the Latin text; it contained two additional books, describing the final conflagration and the new heavens and new earth that are to follow it. Finally this enlarged version was translated into English and published, with further comments by the author, in 1690. The whole work was now entitled *The Theory of the Earth. Containing an Account of the Original of the Earth, and of all the General Changes which it hath already undergone, and is to undergo, till the Consummation of all Things.* The additional books carried a dedication to Queen Mary – appropriately enough, for Burnet enjoyed royal favour for a time, as chaplain in ordinary and clerk of the closet to William III. That was the peak of his career; later, as his writings became more obviously heterodox, he forfeited his appointment and had to withdraw into quiet retirement.

Although in most histories of geology Burnet's book is dismissed as totally unscientific, even as an obstacle to the development of a true geology, there is more to it than that. As a thinker, Burnet had some real merits: he was genuinely curious about the

18   *Right*: Thomas Burnet, by Sir Godfrey Kneller.

19   *Facing page*: The history of the world, from primordial chaos to final conflagration. Frontispiece of Burnet's *Sacred Theory of the Earth*, 1690.

earth's past, and he was able to imagine it as utterly different from its present state. As he himself put it,

> Since I was first inclin'd to the Contemplation of Nature, and took pleasure to trace out the Causes of Effects, and the dependance of one thing upon another in the visible Creation, I had always, methought, a particular curiosity to look back into the Sources and ORIGINAL of things.[6]

In the unexpanded version of his book Burnet's aim was in fact to explain the origins of the earth we live on. In this undertaking he employed, as he puts it, reason as his first guide, and Scripture to confirm and complement the findings of reason. He hoped that his explanation of the Flood as a worldwide catastrophe would make the biblical story more understandable – would not only commend itself to 'all reasonable persons' but would also 'silence the Cavils of Atheists'.

Burnet surveys all the explanations that were current in his time and finds them all inadequate. Yet he cannot accept, either, that

The
Sacred Theory
of the
EARTH.

the Flood was a purely local affair. While approving the usual objections to that theory, he adds one of his own. Much addicted to calculation, he announces that, assuming that human beings in those early times multiplied at the usual rate, 10,737,418,240 people would have been born in the sixteen generations prior to the Flood.[7] So not only Judaea but a great part of the world must have been populated, and a deluge which drowned them all must have been universal. Moreover, in this the earth was conforming to a general pattern, for other planets had floods too. Ancient accounts showed that at the time of Noah Venus was experiencing a flood. The broken surface of Mars indicated that it had gone through a similar cataclysm. On Saturn the polar caps seemed to have fallen into the abyss, no doubt under the impact of a flood.[8]

Still, Burnet's interest was in the biblical Flood, and here he was faced with the problem that had perplexed others before him. He calculated that to cover the mountains to the depth of fifteen cubits, as specified in Genesis, would require at least eight times as much water as was to be found in modern oceans. 'The excessive quantity of water', he tells us, 'is the great difficulty, and the removal of it afterward.'[9] The thought preyed on his mind – until, suddenly, the solution flashed upon him: before the Flood the earth had been quite different from what it was now. In fact, it was perfectly smooth:

> . . . the Face of the Earth before the Deluge was smooth, regular and uniform; without Mountains, and without a Sea . . . An Earth without a Sea, and plain as the *Elysian* fields; if you travel all over, you will not meet with a Mountain or a Rock, yet well provided of all things for an habitable world . . . and so continued for many hundreds of years.[10]

To cover so smooth an earth, Burnet calculated, would require no more water than is now to be found in the oceans. It remained to explain where that water came from – and for that purpose Burnet expounds a whole geogony.[11] The primordial chaos, we are told, consisted of 'the materials and ingredients of all bodies, but mingled in confusion with one another'. The earth came into being when, at God's command, these various elements fell

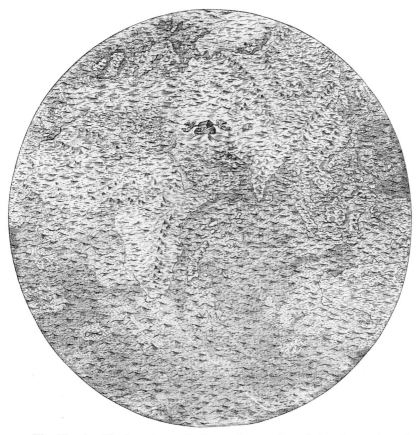

20   The Flood, with the ark watched over by angels and the changed earth
emerging. From *The Sacred Theory of the Earth.*

towards a centre, at rates determined by their specific gravity. The
heaviest element, solid matter, dropped right to the centre, where
it formed a hard core, like the yoke of an egg. Next heaviest was
water; that too moved downwards, to form a sphere around the
solid core. This was 'the *great Abysse*', 'the Sea, or Subterraneous
waters hid in the bowels of the earth'. It also contained oil or
grease, which gradually separated out and floated on the water. As
for the air – that was full of fine particles, which were heavier than
air but lighter than water: these too moved downwards, falling like
snowflakes, until they landed on the oily or greasy surface of the
watery sphere. What resulted was a gummy mass, which in time
was hardened by the action of the sun to become an outer crust of
earth. This crust held the waters as an egg-shell contains the white.

And that, Burnet argued, is what the Psalmist meant when he declared that God 'founded the world upon the seas, and established it upon the rivers', or that he 'spread out the earth upon the waters'.[12]

Burnet has much to say about the primordial earth. In accordance with the perfect nature of God, he argues, the first creation must have been perfect; after all, Genesis itself tells us that God, seeing what he made, pronounced it good. As portrayed in *The Theory of the Earth* the whole of the primordial earth coincided with the terrestrial paradise. That implied that it enjoyed a perfect climate – and so it did. For at that time the earth was always the same distance from the sun; and, since its axis was not yet oblique, it enjoyed perpetual summer. There were no 'violent Meteors there, nor any that proceeded from extremity of Cold; as Ice, Snow, or Hail; nor Thunder neither . . . And as for Winds, they could not be either impetuous or irregular in that Earth . . . Nature was then a stranger to all these disorders.'[13]

The human inhabitants of this perfect world lived in simplicity, purity and innocence. Moreover, the benign atmosphere and the stability of the heavens fostered longevity. Animals and even plants lived very long indeed, and so did human beings: witness the life-spans of the Patriarchs! Conditions were so favourable that human beings, animals and plants all came into existence without parents, being generated spontaneously from the earth – as, Burnet declares, insects and small creeping things still are.

Unfortunately this state of affairs did not last: the benign climate itself proved its undoing.[14] As the sun shone all the year round, much of the subterranean water was turned into vapour, which pressed on the crust. The crust itself dried, cracked and finally split; huge pieces of this ruptured husk fell into the watery layer. The waters, forced upwards, rushed through the cracks and spread over the world. This was the biblical Flood – and in describing it Burnet deploys the full power of his eloquence:

> Thus the Flood came to its height; and 'tis not easy to represent to our selves this strange Scene of things, when the Deluge was in its fury and extremity; when the Earth was broken and swallow'd up in the Abysse, whose raging waters rise higher than the Mountains, and fill'd the Air with broken waves, with

an universal mist, and with thick darkness, so as Nature seem'd
to be in a second Chaos; and upon this Chaos rid the distrest
Ark, that bore the small remains of Mankind. No Sea ever so
tumultuous as this, nor is there any thing in present Nature to
be compar'd with the disorder of these waters . . . The Ark was
really carri'd to the tops of the highest Mountains, and into the
places of the Clouds, and thrown down again into the deepest
Gulfs . . . It was no doubt an extraordinary and miraculous
Providence that could make a Vessel, so ill man'd, live upon
such a Sea; that kept it from being dasht against the Hills, or
overwhelm'd in the Deeps. That Abysse which had devoured
and swallow'd up whole Forests of Woods, Cities and Provinces,
nay the whole Earth, when it had conquer'd all, and triumph'd
over all, could not destroy this single Ship. . . . We may . . . suppose the good Angels to have lookt down upon this ship of
*Noah's*; and that not out of curiosity, as idle spectators, but with
a passionate concern for its safety and deliverance. A Ship,
whose *Cargo* was no less than a whole World; that carry'd the
fortune and hopes of all posterity, and if this had perish'd, the
Earth for any thing we know had been nothing but a Desert, a
great ruine, a dead heap of Rubbish . . .[15]

These things took place at the foreordained time, 1656 years
after Creation. And Burnet, mindful of traditional theology,
explains why: God synchronized the degeneration of mankind
with the natural processes that produced the Flood:

Providence that ruleth all things and all Ages, after the Earth
had stood above sixteen hundred Years, thought fit to put a
period to that World, and accordingly, it was reveal'd to *Noah*,
that for the wickedness and degeneracy of men, God would
destroy mankind from the *Earth* in a Deluge of Water . . . This
seems to me to be the great Art of Divine Providence, so to
adjust the two Worlds, Humane and Natural, Material and
Intellectual, . . . they should all along correspond and fit one
another, and especially in their great Crises and Periods.[16]

In the great crisis that was the Flood the original perfect world
was utterly devastated. Mountains are crumpled bits of the once
smooth crust of the earth, and they are blemishes:

. . . these Mountains are plac'd in no Order one with another, that can either respect use or beauty; And if you consider them singly, they do not consist of any proportion of parts that is referable to any design, or that hath the least Footsteps of Art or Counsel. There is nothing in Nature more shapeless and ill-figur'd than an old Rock or a Mountain, and all that variety that is among them, is but the various modes of irregularity. . . .[17]

Even now the disruption of the primordial uniform whole is still in progress. The earth's crust is still breaking up and sliding into the abyss – that is the meaning of earthquakes.

There are far more massive traces of the great devastation. When the earth's crust broke it split into several huge masses; the edges of these masses fell into the abyss, while the central portions, supported by the inner earth and by the water and air imprisoned there, remained on the surface. These central portions are the present continents and large islands. Parts of the abyss also became ocean beds, into which the waters of the Flood were gradually collected. The Atlantic, the Pacific, the Mediterranean filled great cracks in what was once a single plain. And what they conceal is perhaps the most terrible of all the results of the Flood:

When I present this great Gulf to my imagination, emptied of all its waters, naked and gaping at the Sun, stretching its jaws from one end of the Earth to another, it appears to me the most ghastly thing in Nature.[18]

Like the disruption of the earth's surface, the subsidence of the waters is still in progress. Long after the oceans were formed out of the main body of the Flood, bogs and fens bear witness to the gradual draining of the water from the surface of the earth back into the subterranean abyss.

But things will not remain for ever as they now are. Burnet is as much concerned with the end of the world as with its beginning. The two additional books of *The Theory of the Earth* elaborate on the prophecies in the Second Letter of Peter and the Book of Revelation. Burnet foresees a time when a terrible drought will

dry up the rivers and streams and so desiccate all vegetation that
it could serve only as fuel, adding to the fuel already present in the
stocks of bitumen, sulphur, coal, pitch and oil. All this will then be
ignited at God's command – and the result will be comparable
with the Flood:

> In general, there is a great analogy to be observed betwixt the
> two Deluges, of Water and of Fire ... The Earth ... must be
> reduc'd into a fluid Mass, in the nature of a Chaos, as it was at
> first; but this last will be a Fiery Chaos, as that was a Watery ...[19]

Just as on the eve of the Flood, the heat will transform the
subterranean waters into vapour, which in turn will cause earthquakes and eruptions on sea and land. As a Protestant, Burnet
naturally expects the devastation to start in Italy: Rome will go
under, like Sodom, in a lake of fire and brimstone. The oceans,
already largely evaporated by the heat, will be completely drained,
as all remaining water disappears into the vacated subterranean
cavities and streams of lava flow into the sea bed.

Then the original process of Creation will be repeated. Again
the core of earth will be surrounded by a chaos of air, water and
particles of matter. Again all this will gradually settle on the earth,
to form a smooth crust, without mountains or sea. The primordial
perfect state will return, and this time it will last for just 1,000
years; for Burnet, like many intellectuals of his day, was fascinated
by that famous prophecy in Revelation 20.[20] And as millenarian
fantasies commonly reflect the tastes of those who indulge in
them, it is not surprising that the denizens of the millennial world
will rejoice in 'the Contemplation of God and his Works', including astronomical observation and even 'the theory of humane
nature' – or as we would say, psychology.

From a passage in the Latin version in his book it is clear that
Burnet expected the transformation of the world to take place in
a century or two, and its end to come within 1,500 years. That
end, of course, would coincide with the Last Judgment – after
which the earth would be removed to some other part of the
universe and become a sun or a star.

2

*The Theory of the Earth* represents an ingenious synthesis of two very different bodies of thought: the new, mechanistic cosmology of Descartes and the age-old theological tradition concerning God's curse on the earth.

It seems that Descartes developed his cosmology before the condemnation of Galileo in 1632, but was so shaken by that event that he refrained from publishing his thoughts for many years. And when he did publish them in his *Principia Philosophiae* – in 1644, in Amsterdam, and not in his usual pellucid French but in Latin translation – the work was promptly condemned by the Sorbonne. However, it remained available, and became extremely influential, and was keenly studied by Burnet.

In the fourth part of the *Principia* Descartes describes how in the beginning, as the earth cooled, a hard crust formed around it, and a layer of liquid formed beneath the crust. Next the sun's heat caused the crust to crack, until the earth's surface was ruptured and collapsed upon the inner globe. The result was a welter of irregularities, with some matter falling below the level of the liquid layer, some rising above it; whence the hills and mountains and valleys on the earth's surface, and the hollows in the ocean bed.

The similarity of this geogony to that propounded in *The Theory of the Earth* is obvious: Burnet has followed his celebrated precursor almost step by step. However, he never admitted his debt, but pretended that Descartes had simply arrived at an imperfect understanding of what he himself had come, independently, to understand fully:

> An eminent Philosopher of this Age, Monsieur des Cartes, hath made use of the like Hypothesis to explain the irregular Form of this present Earth, though he never dream'd of the Deluge, nor thought that first Orb, built over the Abyss, to have been any more than a transient Crust, and not a real habitable World that lasted for more than sixteen hundred Years. . . .[21]

It is true that Descartes had no interest in the Flood, but the disagreement went deeper than that. Although Descartes paid lip service to the existence of God as First Cause – as the craftsman who designed the mechanical universe – he allowed him no other function: once set in motion, the universe ran itself. For Descartes the crisis that the universe was supposed to have undergone soon after its formation was to be explained in purely mechanical terms, and so were the visible traces of that crisis. Not so for Burnet. Unlike the French philosopher, the English cleric was a sincere if eccentric Christian. For him the irregularities in the earth's surface were an expression of the wrath of God.

There was nothing original in that notion. For many centuries Jewish expositors of Genesis had maintained that mountains were punishments inflicted on mankind in response to the sin of Adam and Eve, or else of Cain's murder of his brother. Many Christian expositors were equally emphatic, even if they tended to blame these things on the sins of the next generation, that of Adam's grandsons. And some expositors, Jewish and Christian alike, went further. On the strength of an ancient mistranslation of Genesis 3: 17 they maintained that when man sinned he brought misfortune on the whole world. Ever since, the earth itself had suffered under God's curse, and the existence of mountains was a constant reminder of that curse.[22]

However, it was one thing to blame the existence of mountains on the very earliest human beings, and quite another thing to blame it upon the generation of the Flood. For Genesis makes it clear that mountains already existed by that time – did not the Flood cover the mountains, did not the ark rest on a mountain? In the sixteenth and seventeenth centuries the matter was vigorously debated, until a compromise was found. It was argued that even after the Fall mankind continued to degenerate; that nature degenerated along with mankind; that mankind and nature alike were penalized by the Flood; and that mountains, though they had long existed, then became more numerous and inconvenient than they had been before.

In England Godfrey Goodman, a queen's chaplain who was to become Bishop of Gloucester, expressed this view already early in the seventeenth century. His book *The Fall of Man, or The Corruption of Nature*, published first in 1616 and again in 1635, has much to say on the matter. 'As man was corrupted', writes Goodman, '. . . so it stood with the uniformitie of Gods judgments, that noth-

ing should remain untouched, no not the elements themelves.'
The supreme example of a divine judgment was the Flood and
its enduring consequences: 'Hence began a great alteration in
nature, and all things changed to the worst; the earth did decay
in plenty and goodness of fruits . . . So that this generall deluge
was the generall confusion of nature.' Of course there had been
mountains before the Flood, since the ark rested on one. Nevertheless, 'I suppose likewise, that the un-eveness of the earth (the
hils and the vales) were much caused by this generall deluge
. . . for certaine it is, that all the terrible tokens, and signes of Gods
anger and wrath, did accompanie the deluge; and as the waters
did swell above measure, so the billows and waves of the sea did
arise in a wonderfull and fearfull manner; and these (surely)
might well cause a great inequalitie in the earth.'[23]

Such notions were not confined to churchmen: poets such as
Michael Drayton and Edmund Waller were happy to exploit
them.[24] As for Thomas Burnet, he not only adopted them, he
wholly transformed them. It cannot have been easy to fuse the
tragic sense of a world labouring under a divine curse with the
Cartesian sense of a world governed by the interplay of physical
forces. *The Theory of the Earth* is an intellectual *tour de force*.

## 3

*The Theory of the Earth* enjoyed a long vogue. Supplemented by
replies to critics, it was reissued many times in the eighteenth and
early nineteenth centuries (latterly under the title *The Sacred
Theory of the Earth*). The 1719 and later editions carried an ode to
the author, in Latin and in English, by Addison, who had discovered the book as a young man. Now he was free to express
his admiration:

> How strong each Line, each Thought how great,
> With what an energy you rise!
> How shines each Fancy! With what heat
> Does every glowing Page surprize!

Steele was no less enthusiastic: he devoted a complete issue
of *The Spectator* (No. 146) to the book. Later in the eighteenth

century the critic Joseph Warton declared that Burnet 'displayed an imagination very nearly equal to that of Milton'. Wordsworth was delighted to find a passage in the book that harmonized with a passage in *The Excursion*. Coleridge thought of rewriting the book in blank verse, but in the end contented himself with the comment that 'poetry of the highest kind may exist without metre'.[25] Burnet was indeed one of the last great masters of English in the ornate, rhetorical, sonorous baroque mode, and his style has continued to command admiration.

As for the ideas launched by *The Theory of the Earth*, they too had a fascination about them. Isaac Newton himself wrote to Burnet, 'Of our present sea, rocks, mountains etc., I think you have given the most plausible account';[26] while Newton's great antagonist Leibniz, writing within a year of the first general edition of the Latin version of the *Theory*, was happy to adopt Burnet's view of the Flood and its effect on the formation of mountains.[27]

Before long it became a commonplace that the Flood was responsible for much in the present form of the globe, from continents and ocean basins down to hillocks and caves. A number of works published in the 1750s bear witness to the tenacity of the notion. Robert Clayton, Bishop of the Irish diocese of Clogher, maintained, in his *Vindication of the Histories of the Old and New Testaments*, that all the world's ocean basins had been scooped out by the Flood, and that mountains were simply the debris which had accumulated as a result.[28] A Fellow of the Royal Society, Edward Wight, argued that the Flood had swept animal and vegetable debris into huge heaps, which fermented and caught fire; this was the origin of volcanoes.[29] And to a rector of St Lucy's, Barbados, it seemed obvious that the shape of the island's hills was due to battering by the diluvial waters.[30]

# Chapter 6

## *Providential Comets*

1

William Whiston (1667–1752) was a friend, disciple and, in his early years, protégé of Isaac Newton.[1] Already as an undergraduate at Clare Hall, Cambridge, he studied mathematics for eight hours a day, and to such good effect that in 1691 he was elected to a fellowship. At that time Cartesianism was still the dominant form of philosophy, and Whiston studied it – until he read Newton's *Principia* and heard the great man lecture. What happened then was recognized by Whiston himself as a religious conversion – and to a millenarian faith at that. The *Memoirs* which he wrote towards the end of his life contain a striking account of the impact which Newton's discovery of the law of gravity had upon his own thought. This 'noble discovery' was perceived by him as 'an eminent prelude and preparation to those happy times of the restitution of all things, which God has spoken of by the mouth of all his holy prophets, since the world began'.[2]

This double preoccupation, with science and with religion, is very apparent in a book which he produced while he was a Fellow of Clare Hall, and which was published in 1696. The book's title leads one to expect a religious tract: *A New Theory of the Earth from its Original to the Consummation of All Things. Wherin The Creation of the World in Six days, The Universal Deluge, And the General Conflagration, As laid down in the Holy Scriptures, Are shown to be perfectly agreeable to Reason and Philosophy*. The form of the work, on the other hand, is that of a mathematical treatise: Book I consisting of Lemmata, Book II of Hypotheses, Book III of 'Phaenomena', and Book IV of Solutions, or applications to the phenomena of the principles expressed. Significantly, the manuscript had been 'laid before Sir *Isaac Newton* himself, on whose Principles it depended, and who well approved of it'.[3]

A couple of years later, Whiston, who had been ordained before taking up his fellowship, was awarded the living of Lowestoft, and happily settled down to be the zealous vicar of what was then a small fishing village. But in 1701 Newton, who had been appointed Warden of the Mint in London, arranged for Whiston to succeed him as Lucasian Professor of Mathematics at Cambridge.

For nine years Whiston pursued an energetic academic career, giving public university lectures on astronomy and mathematics and also writing and publishing works on biblical exegesis and on the history of Christian doctrine. In his religious as much as in his scientific concern he was following in Newton's footsteps – but it ruined his career. Whiston became convinced that the doctrine of the Trinity was a false accretion to primitive Christianity: neither Christ himself nor his early followers had believed that the Son was consubstantial with the Father. Privately, Newton had reached the same conclusion; but his native caution and his concern for his social position prevented him from announcing the fact. Whiston, for his part, was incapable of temporizing, was indeed heroically outspoken; and his antitrinitarian lectures and publications not only cost him his professorship but ensured his banishment from the University.

In 1710, at the age of forty-three, with a wife and three children to support, Whiston began a new career as a freelance writer and lecturer on astronomy, on primitive Christianity, and on the imminent fulfilment of the biblical prophecies. Forty years later he was still touring the country, proclaiming the imminence of the Second Coming and the Millennium, and illustrating his argument with a model of Ezekiel's eschatological Temple.

Long before that, Whiston had come to be ridiculed as a religious eccentric. His *New Theory of the Earth*, on the other hand, had an illustrious career. When it first appeared, no less a person that John Locke commented that Whiston had 'explained

21    *Right*: William Whiston, 1720. Artist
unknown.

22    *Facing page*: A gathering of eminent
persons at Tunbridge Wells, including
Dr Johnson, his wife, and his friend Mrs
Thrale; the dramatist Colley Cibber; the
actor David Garrick; and the Prime
Minister William Pitt the Elder, Earl of
Chatham. Whiston is in the right-hand
corner, characteristically turning his back
on the company and making off.

so many wonderful, and before inexplicable Things in the
great Changes of this Globe'; and he noted that amongst his
acquaintances the book was universally praised.[4] It long remained
influential – it had six editions in all, the last in 1755. Nor was its
fame confined to England. When in 1728 the philosopher Bishop
Berkeley tried to establish a college in Bermuda for the training of
clergymen and the education of the Indians, one of the books he
brought with him was a copy of the *New Theory*; and when the
scheme failed, this volume, along with the rest of the library, went
to Yale, where it deeply influenced the thinking of the President
of Yale, Ezra Stiles. As late as 1742 the rector of a German university produced a book based on the *New Theory*. In France around
the same time Whiston's book influenced thinkers of the stature
of Maupertuis.[5]

And wherever Whiston's *New Theory of the Earth* became known,
people were fascinated by his interpretation of the Flood.

2

Whiston was of course familiar with Burnet's *Theory of the Earth* – in fact he had offered a vindication of that work as part of the exercises for his first degree at Cambridge, and he continued to share many of Burnet's views. But he had his reservations: Burnet had played fast and loose with the text of Genesis; in particular, he had underestimated the role of what was known as 'special Providence', or the sudden, miraculous interference of God in the normal course of things. To Whiston – and to Newton – these were grievous errors. Moreover, even in terms of Newtonian physics Burnet's account of the early history of the earth was manifestly wrong.[6] That was why *A New Theory of the Earth* was called for.

As a professional astronomer, Whiston was much preoccupied with comets. In fact he was convinced that originally the earth itself had been a comet. Some six or seven thousand years ago that comet had been changed, by God's decision, into a planet ideally suited to sustain life – and so it had remained until it was interfered with by another comet.

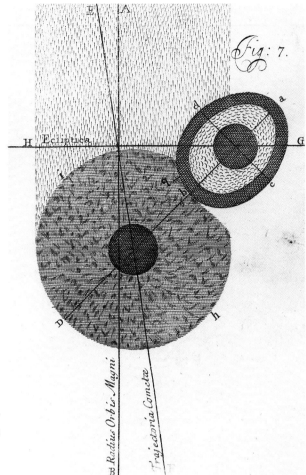

Fig: 7.

23　A diagram from *A New Theory of the Earth*, 1696, intended to illustrate in a scientific manner the disastrous effects of the passage of Halley's comet.

Whiston was no less certain than Burnet that the earth before the Flood was incomparably superior to the earth we know. The sun's course was such that the earth's inhabitants enjoyed a perpetual equinox. Moreover the orbits of the planets and the earth were perfect circles, and the sun was at the centre of the earth's orbit. The orbit of the moon was isochronic with that of the earth, so that a lunar month was the same as a solar month. A day was as long as one of our present years – which meant that the 'six days' of creation were really six years. The earth was far more fertile, and accordingly was able to support a vastly larger population, both of animals and of human beings, than it does now.[7] The air was 'thin, pure, subtile and homogeneous', 'free from violent winds, storms and agitations' – with the result that people all lived much longer, often up to a thousand years.[8]

Unfortunately all these happy circumstances were upset by a comet – which Whiston finally identified as Halley's – passing near the earth. The present orbits started then. And that event could be dated: it occurred in 2349 BCE. This date was often given as that of the Flood, and Whiston was prepared to be more precise: the Flood began on 28 November of that year. In fact it was the comet that caused the Flood, and Whiston describes how it did so. A comet carries vapours with it in its atmosphere, and 'rarified and expanded' vapours in its tail. The rest follows:

> If we consider that a comet . . . is capable of passing so close by the Body of the Earth as to involve it in its *Atmosphere* and *Tail* a considerable time, and leave prodigious quantities of the same Condensed and Expanded Vapours upon its Surface; we shall easily see that a Deluge of Waters is by no means an impossible thing.[9]

At the same time the pressure of water caused fissures in the earth's crust, through which the waters within the globe were ejected, to add to the Flood.

One problem remained. According to Genesis, Noah entered the ark on the day the rains began; why, then, was he not swept away in the torrents launched by the comet? Whiston had his answer ready. The comet descended at the Garden of Eden, and the ark was situated somewhat to the east of that point. So Noah had nearly twenty-four hours to spare before the earth's rotation brought him into full torrent – by which time he was safe inside the ark.

The comet was the means by which God brought the Flood about. For Whiston never doubts that 'the Deluge of Waters was a sign and instance of the Divine Vengeance on a wicked World, and was the effect of the peculiar and extraordinary Providence of God'.[10] And he elaborates:

> That exactly at a time which was fit and proper, and in an Age that justly deserved so great a Judgment, the Comet shou'd come by, and overwhelm the World, is very remarkably and

extraordinarily the Finger of God Himself. That Omniscient Being, who foresaw when the degeneracy of Human Nature wou'd be arrived at an *insufferable* degree of Wickedness, the Iniquities of the World wou'd be compleatly *full*; and when consequently his Vengeance ought to fall upon them, praedisposed and praeadapted the Orbits and Motions of both the Comet and the Earth, so that at that very time, and only at that time, the former shou'd pass close by the latter, and bring that dreadful Punishment upon them. Had not God Almighty on purpose thus adjusted the Moments and Courses of each, 'twere infinite odds that such a Conjunction and Coincidence of a Comet and a Planet, wou'd have happen'd during the whole space, between the Creation and the Conflagration of this World; much more at such a critical Point of time when Mankind, by their unparallel'd Wickedness were deserving of . . . no less than almost an *Utter Extinction*.[11]

So the Flood described in Genesis is not only 'fully account-able', it is 'almost demonstrable'. And it was a true cataclysm. Whiston was able to calculate the average depth of the water covering the earth: 10,821 feet – which, allowing for the fact that much of the earth's surface is occupied by mountains, would be enough water to submerge everything, including the highest mountains. It took centuries for the water to drain off the earth's surface, and even then much remained: it is thanks to the Flood that the habitable part of the globe is divided into two vast conti-nents separated by an ocean.[12]

The long-term consequences of the Flood were in every way disastrous – though no more so than was appropriate to the fallen state of mankind. The weight of the liquid from the comet changed the length of the solar year, increasing it by five days, and of the month, which was shortened, with the result that the calendar has been incoherent ever since. The original surface of the earth was covered over by fresh strata and became inaccessible to mankind; and the present surface, newly acquired after the Flood, is far less fertile.[13] The atmosphere became less temperate – indeed, it became 'full of Exhalations, Nitrosulphureous, or other Heterogeneous Mixtures, as occasion Coruscations, Meteors, Thunder, Lightning, with Contagious and Pestilential Infections . . . and have so very pernicious and fatal (tho' almost insensible) Effects in the World'.[14]

The final conflagration will likewise be produced by a comet. Either a comet will draw the earth out of its orbit, so that it will be burned up by the sun, or else it will dry up all the water and heat the earth's air until it becomes as hot as the comet's own atmosphere. However, the water of the abyss will remain; and after the earth's crust has been reduced to chaos, it will reconsolidate on that same abyss, and become again as it was in the time before the Flood, perhaps even like Paradise before the Fall.[15] The earth's diurnal course will be retarded until it corresponds exactly with its annual course in its orbit. Since there will no longer be any succession of days and nights, there will be no need for sun or moon; instead, there will be perpetual day, lit by supernatural light. And there will be no sea.

No less steeped in millenarian teachings than Burnet, Whiston expected the earth to pass into 'a new State, proper to receive the Saints and Martyrs for its Inhabitants'.[16] He knew, too, that at the end of the fated thousand years the Last Judgment would come, and the consummation of all things; after which – as Burnet also claimed – the earth would be removed from its present position and leave the solar system.[17] Naturally, Whiston expected this change to be effected by a comet, and he also expected the earth to become a comet itself – whereas Burnet expected it to become a star.

Not surprisingly, both Burnet's and Whiston's interpretations of the Flood, though widely praised, also met with many objections. A representative sample of those objections is given in the Appendix.


### 3

Whiston was not the only thinker who tried to interpret the Flood in terms of cometary interference. In December 1694, a year and a half before the publication of *A New Theory of the Earth*, the astronomer Edmund Halley read two papers at meetings of the Royal Society, entitled respectively 'Some Considerations about the Cause of the universal Deluge' and 'Some farther Thoughts upon the same Subject'. Here he argued that when God, as 'the author of this dreadful execution upon mankind', dictated the story to Moses for incorporation into Genesis, he must have concealed much concerning the natural processes involved: the references to forty days and nights of rain, and to waters rising from the bowels of the earth, were insufficient to explain a worldwide inundation. Halley suggests, instead, 'the casual *choc* of a *comet*, or other transient body'. His account of what would have followed from such an impact deserves to be quoted in full:

> . . . the great Agitation such a *Choc* must necessarily occasion in the Sea [would be] sufficient to answer for all those strange Appearances of heaping vast Quantities of Earth and high Cliffs upon Beds of Shells, which once were the Bottom of the Sea; and raising up Mountains where none were before, mixing the Elements into such a Heap as the Poets describe the *old Chaos*; for such a *Choc* impelling the solid Parts would occasion the Waters, and all fluid Substances that were unconfined, as the Sea is, with one *Impetus* to run violently towards that Part of the Globe where the Blow was received; and that with Force sufficient to take with it the whole Bottom of the Ocean, and to carry it upon the land; heaping up into Mountains those earthy Parts it had born away with it, in those Places where the opposite Waves balance each other . . . which may account for those long continued Ridges of Mountains. And again, the Recoil of this Heap of Waters would return towards the opposite Parts of the Earth, with a lesser *Impetus* than the first, and so reciprocating many times, would at last come to settle in such a Manner as we now observe in the Structure of the superficial Parts of the Globe.
>
> In this case it will be much more difficult to shew how *Noah* and the *Animals* should be preserved, than that all things in which was the Breath of Life, should hereby be destroyed. Such a *Choc* would also occasion a differing Length of the Day and Year, and change the Axis of the Globe . . . That some such thing has happened, may be guess'd, for that the Earth seems as if it were new made out of the Ruins of an old World, wherein appear such Animal Bodies as were before the Deluge, but . . . have endured ever since, either petrified, or else entire . . .

In his second paper Halley produces even more remarkable thoughts. Perhaps, he says, these things happened not at the time

24 Edmund Halley, by
Thomas Murray.

of the Flood, some four thousand years ago, but much earlier,
before man was created. Such 'agitations' may even have befallen
this globe not once but many times. And they may recur in future
'in due Periods of Time'. It may even be that such periodical
catastrophes are necessary, so that the world shall receive a fresh
new surface when the old surface has been used up and can no
longer sustain life. Halley concludes with a sobering reflection:
'This may be thought hard, to destroy the whole Race for the
Benefit of those that are to succeed' – but then the life of each
individual is so short that it hardly matters when one dies.

Though Whiston apparently knew of Halley's papers, in
general they made no stir. Apprehensive, as he himself admits, of
incurring ecclesiastical censure, Halley refused to have them published at the time, and deposited them in the archives of the Royal
Society. And when they were at last published, in 1725, they

attracted no more attention than one would expect of half a dozen pages buried in volume 39 of the Society's *Philosophical Transactions*.

Halley clearly accepted that the Flood really happened, and it was while reflecting on what he calls 'the strange catastrophe' that these thoughts came to him. They are astonishing thoughts. That from time to time a comet or other 'transient object' may have struck the earth, destroying whole 'races'; that life has nevertheless always survived, to flourish anew; that this process may well recur in future – such thoughts are familiar to astrophysicists and geologists today. In 1690 they were very strange – which no doubt is why they passed almost unnoticed.

Meanwhile another line of speculation had opened up – one which was to lead, eventually, in the same direction. How was it that fossils of sea creatures were to be found far inland? Was the Flood responsible for that? Or . . . ?

# Chapter 7

## *Problematic Fossils*

### 1

Often hundreds of miles from the sea, sometimes high in the mountains, sometimes embedded in rocks, there they were: stony objects that looked like the shells of marine molluscs or the teeth of sharks or even entire fish. What could they be? And how could they have got where they were?[1]

Down the centuries many answers to those questions had been advanced – when an eighteenth-century scholar set about listing them, he found a round dozen.[2] There had always been some who accepted the 'marine-mountainous bodies' as the remains of once-living sea creatures, and others who regarded them as mere imitations – sports of Nature in her playful mood; or maybe as attempts by the land to rival the sea in fertility. Amongst those who took fossils at face value, some held that they were the debris of ancient picnics, or even that they had been carried to the mountain-tops by the wind. Others – from Leonardo da Vinci in the fifteenth century to Robert Hooke in the seventeenth – came nearer to the truth, arguing that in some parts of the earth what was now dry land had once been covered by sea.

But there were always those – from Tertullian in the second century onwards[3] – who were convinced that sea creatures had been carried to the mountain-tops by the Flood, and left stranded there when it withdrew. It was not an unreasonable assumption for people who could not possibly know that fossils are to be

NICOLAVS STENONIVS

25   Nicolaus Steno. Artist
unknown.

found, arranged in an orderly fashion, layer upon layer, for many
thousand feet down in solid rock. And it was encouraging to find
such a striking corroboration of the biblical story of the Flood:
here was proof enough that the earth had indeed been submerged after the creation of animal life.

   In the late seventeenth century the diluvial origin of fossils
seemed to find scientific confirmation. The thinker who inte-
grated the traditional belief into the new mechanistic world-view
was a Dane called Niels Stensen (1638–86); in his day his name
was Latinized to Stenonius, and in English-speaking countries he
is usually known as Steno.[4] Steno had started as an anatomist and
in that capacity he had acquired an international reputation while
still in his early twenties. When dissecting a sheep's head he
discovered the outlet of the parotid gland – which is why it is
called the *ductus Stenonianus*. His work on the brain and the heart
resulted in contributions of lasting importance. When, at the age
of twenty-eight, he arrived in Florence his fame was such that
he was appointed physician to the Grand Duke of Tuscany,

Ferdinand II, and was also given a hospital post which allowed him ample time for research.

The first turning-point in his extraordinary career came when, as a member of the Accademia del Cimento, the academy for experimentation, he was called upon to dissect the head of a huge shark. Strange objects known as *glossopetrae* or 'tongue-stones' were constantly being found embedded in rocks, and it was widely assumed that rocks were as constantly producing them. Moreover these objects were credited with medicinal and magical powers. When Steno examined the head of his shark he came to suspect that, so far from being new and extraordinary pieces of rock, *glossopetrae* were the fossilised teeth of sharks that had lived and died long, long ago. He wrote up his argument and published it in 1667 in an excessively modest form – as an appendix to an anatomical study. It nevertheless attracted enough attention for the Secretary of the Royal Society in London, Henry Oldenburg, to produce an abstract for the Society's *Philosophical Transactions.*

Steno was deeply stirred by what he seemed to be discovering. He undertook excavations, in Tuscany and elsewhere. He planned to write a full-scale work on fossils, in Latin, to be entitled *De Solido Intra Solidum Naturaliter Contento. (On Solids Naturally Enclosed Within Other Solids.)* However, he never wrote it, for he had reached a second turning-point. Always a deeply religious man, in Florence he abandoned his native Lutheranism for Catholicism – his conversion being completed, in 1667, by a mystical experience as overwhelming as that of his near-contemporary Blaise Pascal. In 1675 he was ordained priest. Later he served for a time as suffragan to the Bishop of Münster in Westphalia, and he ended his days as a missionary in the remote Protestant town of Schwerin in Mecklenburg. Throughout his priestly career he lived a rigorously ascetic life, refusing all grand vestments, fasting much, giving all his money to the poor. It was a hard life, and his letters showed that he often longed for the peace and friendships he had enjoyed in Italy. And though he wrote a number of theological works, after his ordination he never wrote a word about science.

That does not mean that he felt his religion and his science to be in conflict. On the contrary, like many others in his day he regarded his scientific work as illustrating the wonders of the

Creator's handiwork. His attitude is admirably conveyed by a celebrated Latin sentence of his, which in translation reads:

> Lovely are the things we see, i.e. the human body's surface; lovelier is what we have come to know: the ingenious arrangement of the whole body, the mind which has so many and such masterly resources at its disposal; but by far the loveliest is what we cannot know: the dependence of all these things upon the Cause who knows all that of which we are ignorant.[5]

What Steno says here of his researches in anatomy was no less true of his work in the earth-sciences. It was no revulsion from science but a total commitment to his priestly vocation that ended his career as an intellectual pioneer. Moreover, though he never wrote his great work on fossils, he did produce – in 1669, after his conversion but before his ordination – an essay known as the *Prodromus*, or 'Forerunner' – in effect, a sketch for the great work.[6] With this astonishing little book Steno founded three new sciences – geology, palaeontology and crystallography.

In the *Prodromus* the notion of stratification is formulated for the first time. During his excavations Steno had found that the rock formations of Tuscany consisted of a number of strata; and he rightly concluded that this must be true of the earth's crust everywhere. In the *Prodromus* he argues that these strata must originally have been deposited in horizontal layers; the tilted position in which they are now usually found must have resulted from subsequent upheavals. Stratification therefore pointed to a sequence of events in the history of the earth. The shark's teeth, the shells of molluscs and the rest must have been lodged within the sediment as it was deposited layer by layer. Furthermore – and it was a truly amazing insight – Steno argued that as the lower, earlier strata – such as the slaty rocks which he had found in the Apennines – contained no fossils, they must have been laid down before the beginnings of life.

Steno's main inspiration certainly came from his excavations and observations. But, like so many thinkers of his time, he was also much influenced by the speculations in Descartes' *Principia Philosophiae*. Albeit at a very different intellectual level, he was no less willing than Thomas Burnet to make the Cartesian geogony

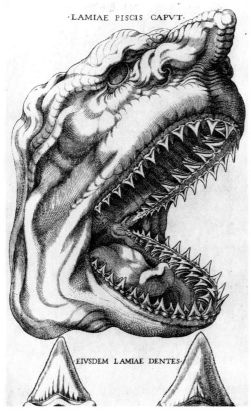

·LAMIAE PISCIS CAPVT·

·EIVSDEM LAMIAE DENTES·

26 The shark's head which led Steno to his decoding of the glossopetrae and so to his discovery of stratification.

his own. He too was persuaded that the primordial earth had a smooth surface, which covered a sphere of water; and that it was the collapse of the earth's crust into the subterranean waters that had given the earth its present uneven surface. When he describes the mechanism of stratal collapse and the formation of tilted strata, he comes very close to Descartes' diagrammatic representation. And when he dates the oldest, fossil-free strata to the earth's first beginnings, he explicitly agrees with Descartes.[7]

But – again like Burnet – Steno was concerned to reconcile Cartesian theory with scriptural chronology. Like practically everybody else at that time, he took the biblical time-scale for granted: he had no reason to suspect that the earth might be older than six thousand years or so. Even when he worked out a scheme of six periods in the earth's history, he had no difficulty in fitting those periods into six thousand years.

Steno was particularly gratified to find a chain of evidence which seemed to show that some of his fossils dated from the time of the Flood. He pointed out that blocks of stone in the oldest walls of the Etruscan city of Volterra contained fossil shells. Volterra was built at least three thousand years ago – and that was almost as long ago as the date at which, according to the chronologists, the Flood had taken place. And Steno went further. The fossiliferous strata, he insisted, must have been deposited by the Flood. Of all events known to history, only the Flood was violent enough to have lifted these strata high above the present sea-level.[8]

That a universal Flood had really occurred was certain, for Scripture said so. But Steno could not rest content with that: many years before Burnet and Whiston, he set about proving that the biblical account was wholly compatible with the new mechanistic science. In the *Prodromus* he argues that the Flood was caused by the concomitant action of a variety of natural causes. When the earth's crust collapsed, fragments blocked the passages through which, it was believed, the sea sent water to springs on the surface – so the sea overflowed. Caverns beneath the sea-floor expanded, forcing the floor upwards – again making the sea overflow. The fire at the earth's centre drove the waters of the subterranean layer upwards, on to the earth's surface. Rain fell incessantly, washing soil down into the cavities on the earth's surface and filling them up. So the waters from the abyss, from the sea, from the sky flooded over the earth – all the more easily because the earth's surface was still flat. In all this, Steno adds, 'there is nothing opposed to Scripture, or reason, or daily experience'.[9]

Two centuries after Steno's death, Thomas Huxley, in an address to a meeting of the British Association, remarked that the correct interpretation of fossils had begun with Steno: 'The principles of investigation thus excellently stated and illustrated by Steno in 1669, are those which have, consciously or unconsciously, guided the researches of palaeontologists ever since.'[10] True enough – yet in Steno's own mind the correct interpretation of fossils was impossible without reference to the Flood.

That was still the case with his immediate successors, John Woodward in England and Johann Scheuchzer in Switzerland.

27    John Woodward, *c.*1710.
Artist unknown.

2

One is not likely in a lifetime to come across anyone like Steno –
a scientific genius who is also a saint. On the other hand anyone
who has lived much in academic circles will recognize John
Woodward as belonging to a familiar type: clever, but no genius
except in his own opinion; intolerant of disagreement and unfor-
giving of criticism; uneasy at any hint of competition; discour-
teous to the point of boorishness; generally disliked, and mocked
whenever opportunity offers. However, Woodward was at least an
indefatigable researcher and a lively writer, and his ideas about
fossils and the Flood had a wide resonance.

Woodward (1665 or 1668–1728) was a self-made man.[11] Born
in a Derbyshire village, he was sent to London as an apprentice to
a linen draper. Somehow he came to the notice of the king's

physician, who removed him from the drapery and took him into his own household. There Woodward received both a medical training and a wide-ranging general education, from which he profited so well that at the age of twenty-seven (at most) he was appointed Professor of Physick (i.e. medicine) at Gresham College in London. He remained comfortably lodged at the College for the rest of his life, with a busy and varied practice.

Yet it was not as a physician that Woodward was best known. Before he even embarked on his medical career he made, at Sherborne in Gloucestershire, a discovery that was to influence the rest of his life: shellfish lodged in solid rock, and whole beds of shells in the ploughed fields. 'This was a speculation new to me', he wrote later, 'and that I judj'd of so great moment that I resolved to pursue it through all the remoter parts of the Kingdom.'[12] And so he did, climbing about in quarries and delving into mines, always making close observations, and gradually building up an impressive collection of specimens. By the time he began his medical practice he was also an expert on fossils and an acknowledged authority in the nascent sciences of geology and palaeontology. It was not for nothing that, in the same year as he was appointed Professor of Physick, he was elected to the Royal Society.

In 1695, when he was at most twenty-eight, Woodward produced the book that made him famous: *An Essay toward a Natural History of the Earth: and Terrestrial Bodies, especially Minerals: As also of the Sea, Rivers, and Springs. With an Account of the Universal Deluge: and of the Effects that it had upon the Earth.* In this work the Flood and its consequences are described in uniquely radical terms – more radical than anything to be found even in Burnet's *Theory of the Earth.*

In Woodward's view the Flood produced a total dissolution of the earth's crust, so that no trace is now left of the ante-diluvian world:

Here was, we see, a mighty Revolution; and *that* attended with Accidents very strange and amazing: the most horrible and portentous Catastrophe that Nature ever saw: an elegant, orderly and habitable Earth quite unhinged, shattered all to pieces, and turned into an heap of ruins: Convulsions so exor-

28 Vain Speculation (in the background) being disabused by Sound Judgment about the true nature of fossils. Title-page of a book by Agostino Scilla, 1670.

bitant and unruly: a Change so exceeding great and violent, that the very Representation alone is enough to startle and shock a Man. In truth the thing, at first, appeared so wonderful and surprizing to me, that I must confess I was for some time at a stand . . .[13]

What persuaded Woodward that all this had really occurred was a careful consideration of marine fossils and their surroundings. These objects, he points out, were to be found 'incorporated with and lodged in all sorts of Stone, in Marble, in Chalk, and . . . in all other ordinary Matter of the Globe which is close and compact enough to preserve them' – and not only here and there but 'in all parts of the known World, as well in Europe, Africa, and America, as in Asia, and this even to the tops of the highest Mountains'.[14] Only a world-shattering cataclysm could account for these extraordinary facts.

Woodward was quite clear about the processes involved. Like so many others, he was convinced that beneath the earth's crust there lay an orb of water, encircling the earth, and connected by numerous passages with the bottom of the sea. He was also convinced that the amount of water in that 'abyss' (he uses the biblical term) was enough, if brought to the surface, to swamp the whole globe, including the highest mountains.[15] At the time of the Flood those waters had indeed been brought up through breaches in the earth's crust. Next, all solid substances in the earth's crust were dissolved to become 'one common confused Mass'.

But how was all this possible? Woodward's ideas on that subject developed over the years; the final version is given in a letter addressed to the President of the Royal Society, Sir Robert Southwell, and appended to *A Supplement and Continuation* of the *Essay* published in 1714. Thanks to Newton's great work Woodward had come to recognize that solid bodies owe their cohesion to gravity, and that if gravity were wholly suspended, everything would dissolve. Clearly, that had never happened – but why should 'the Hand of the supreme Governor of the Universe' not have effected a simple diminution of gravity, so that the earth's crust became an amorphous mass, suspended in the waters of the Flood? Then, when the full force of gravity was restored, 'the globe [would be] finished and formed anew'.

However, in all this only solid matter would have been involved. 'The Parts of Vegetables and Animals would not be affected in the least. The Fibres, of which they are composed would [not] untwist, unweave, or untye, on the Suspension of Gravity . . .' Which is why the remains of plants and marine creatures and other living beings survived, as sole remants of the world before the Flood.

To return to the original *Essay*: As the Flood subsided all things sank down towards the centre of the earth, more or less deeply according to their specific gravity. This accounted both for stratification and for fossils. As the various kinds of matter began to re-form, the heavier kinds, such as stone, sank farthest, and so did the heavier kind of marine creatures – which is why both are found together. Because of their weight the shells of periwinkles and scallops sank farthest, and were concreted with marble; the shells of sea-urchins reached only the lighter, chalky strata; while still lighter shells, of lobsters and the like, were simply absorbed without trace into the fertile humus.[16] Or so – mistakenly of course – Woodward believed.

Originally all these shells were deposited in parallel strata in a smooth earth; but at some time towards the end of the Flood a complication occurred. Heat within the earth caused some strata to rise, while others sank: so mountains and valleys and islands come into being.[17] This last notion is reminiscent of *The Theory of the Earth*, but whatever debt Woodward owed to Burnet remained unacknowledged. In fact the book ends with an attack on Burnet, delivered with characteristic arrogance.

Woodward nevertheless had much in common with Burnet, and with Whiston, and indeed with all those English scientists of the time who felt that in studying nature they were studying the unfolding of the divine plan.[18] It was perhaps no coincidence that he received a doctorate in medicine from Cambridge University, that centre of Latitudinarian thinking; or that by his will he endowed a professorship at Cambridge, and left his great collection of fossils to the University – where it can still be inspected today in the Woodward Museum, which is part of the Sedgwick Museum of Geology.

In Woodward's view the Flood was a miracle; in his own words, 'as the System of Nature was then, and still is, supported and established, a Deluge neither could then, nor can now, happen naturally.'[19] It was God who let the waters loose from the abyss, and he did so in pursuance of a divine plan whose ultimate aim was the good of mankind.

On occasion Woodward could rival Burnet in his handling of that splendid instrument, seventeenth-century English – which would seem to justify a generous use of direct quotation in his case also. Certainly the wonderfully intricate yet perfectly clear sentence in which he defines the true meaning of the Flood could only lose by editing:

And though the whole Series of this extraordinary *Turn* may seem at first view to exhibit nothing but Tumult and Disorder:

nothing but hurry, jarring, and distraction of things: though it may carry along with it some slight shew that 'twas managed blindly and at random: yet if we draw somewhat nearer, and take a closer prospect of it: if we look into its retired Movements, and more secret and latent Springs, we may there trace out a steady Hand, producing good out of evil: the most consummate and absolute Order and Beauty, out of the highest Confusion and Deformity: acting with the most exquisite Contrivance and Wisdom: attending vigilantly throughout the whole Course of this grand Affair, and directing all the several Steps and Periods of it to *an End*, and that a most noble and excellent one; no less than the Happiness of the whole race of Mankind, of all the many Generations of Men which were to come after: which were to inhabit this Earth, thus moduled anew, thus suited to their present Condition and Necessities.[20]

It follows that the purpose of the Flood was something more than the punishment of a sinful mankind. That could have been achieved 'without this ransacking of Nature, and turning all things topsie-turvy: without this battering of the Earth, and unhinging the whole frame of the Globe'.[21] Mankind could have been reduced to a handful by means of wars, famines, local floods, meteorites – but that would have solved nothing. So long as the conditions of life remained the same, 'every Age would have lain under fresh Inducements to the same Crimes: and there would have been a new necessity to punish and reclaim the World: to depopulate the Earth, and reduce it again to a vast Solitude, as constantly as there succeeded a new Age and Race of Men.'[22]

God's plan was deeper: ''tis very plain that the Deluge was not sent only as an Executioner to Mankind: but that its prime Errand was to reform and *new-mold the Earth*.'[23] A new earth was created 'more nearly accommodated to the present frailties of its Inhabitants'.[24] For the ante-diluvian world was boundlessly fertile – so fertile that it never needed to be ploughed, or cultivated in any way. This was wholly appropriate to mankind in its original state of perfection – but wholly inappropriate to the state of mankind after the Fall. Genesis tells us how far Mankind had degenerated by the eve of the Flood – and Woodward explains why this was bound to happen: '. . . now these exuberant Productions of the earth became a continual Decoy and Snare unto him . . . gave him leisure to contrive, and full swing to pursue his Follies; by which means he was laid open to all manner of Pravity, Corruption, and Enormity.'[25] Precisely because there was no need to work, 'the World was little better than a common fold of Phrenticks and Bedlams'.[26]

But then God intervened: 'to reclaim and retrieve the World out of this wretched and forlorn state, the common Father and Benefactor of Mankind seasonably interposed his hand: and rescued miserable Man out of the gross Stupidity and Sensuality whereinto he was thus unfortunately plunged.'[27] God's instrument for effecting this great change was the Flood, which not only dissolved the fertile crust of the existing earth but replaced it by one requiring constant labour – and which even then would only barely support mankind.

Woodward summarizes and concludes his argument with a grand peroration:

> For the *Destruction* of the *Earth* was not only an Act of the profoundest Wisdom and Forecast, but the most monumental proof that could ever possibly have been, of Goodness, Compassion, and Tenderness, in the Author of our Being; and *this* so liberal too and extensive, as to reach all the succeeding Ages of Mankind: all the Posterity of *Noah*: all that should dwell upon the thus renewed Earth to the End of the World; by this means removing the old Charm: the Bait that had so long bewildered and deluded unhappy Man; setting him once more upon his Legs: reducing him from the most abject and stupid Ferity, to his Senses, and to sober Reason: from the most deplorable Misery and Slavery, to a Capacity of being happy.[28]

It is, one feels, the wisdom of a man who owed his success to his own enterprise and energy, and who through all the vicissitudes of his life (including many self-inflicted ones) never stopped working.

The *Essay* was much criticized, though more on scientific than on theological grounds. Nobody doubted Woodward's knowledge of fossils, but his more wide-ranging theories roused misgivings. The great naturalist John Ray saw clearly that the account of the Flood and its consequences was no more than a conjecture presented with unjustified dogmatism. Others pointed to observable facts that contradicted that account: for instance, the heaviest fossil shells were often found not deep buried but on the surface. The assertion that the earth's crust had been totally dissolved seemed particularly unconvincing – for if it had been, how could mere shells have survived intact? And how, in any case, could marine creatures have been destroyed by a deluge of their own element?

Especially damaging was a pamphlet by the eminent mathematician and medical doctor John Arbuthnot, published in 1697. This drew attention to the lack of explanation in Woodward's scheme. How, after the Flood, had the mass of water returned to the abyss? Why had the dissolved matter not disappeared with it, instead of turning into solid strata? And why had the strata become solid at all? Arbuthnot even claimed to have disproved Woodward's theory by laboratory tests: if an oyster-shell and an equal weight of metal powder were thrown into water together, the oyster-shell was the first to sink, despite its lower specific gravity.

That was not all. The title of Arbuthnot's pamphlet was *An Examination of Dr. Woodward's Account of the Deluge . . . With a Comparison of Steno's Philosophy and the Doctor's, in the Case of Marine Bodies dug out of the Earth*. Woodward had nowhere acknowledged any debt to Steno, but here were extracts from Woodward's *Essay* interleaved with extracts from Steno's *Prodromus*, and there could be no doubt about it: Woodward had not only read the great scientist's work, he had plagiarized it.

However, that plagiarism may have rendered a service, not indeed to Steno (who was long since dead) but to Steno's ideas. Whereas Steno's *Prodromus* was known only to a restricted circle of scientists, Woodward's *Essay* – despite all the criticism it had called forth – quickly became famous, and was even translated into Latin, French, Italian and German. And wherever it was read people became acquainted not only with Woodward's own fanciful speculations but with Steno's great discovery of stratification.

### 3

Woodward had one friend who was so devoted and admiring that it was impossible to quarrel with him: the Swiss naturalist

29  Johann Scheuchzer. From his *Herbarium Diluvanium*, 1723.

Johann Jakob Scheuchzer (1672–1733).[29] Scheuchzer started to collect fossils while still a student. Established as a physician and teacher of mathematics in his native city of Zurich, he launched a weekly journal of natural history and began to publish papers on fossils. At that time he still believed fossils to be *lusus naturae*, mere sports of nature, which might look like the remains of once-living creatures but which were really inorganic mineral formations. That was still his view when he produced his first work on fossils, the *Specimen Lithographiae Helvetiae Curiosae*, in 1702. But when he read Woodward's *Essay*, everything changed.

Scheuchzer was immediately converted. To give Woodward's ideas wider currency on the Continent he translated the *Essay* into Latin; the translation was published in 1704. He also set about re-examining and reinterpreting the fossils in his collection. It was obvious to him now that what he had collected as a student in

Germany, and later around the shores of Lake Constance, were the petrified remains of creatures than once lived in the sea. It was obvious, also, how they come to be where he found them: the Flood had brought them there. Following Woodward, Scheuchzer declared that the Flood had converted the earth's crust into a fluid jelly, which later solidified. The proof was there, in those indisputable relics of the Flood, the snails, sea-shells, fish and plants embedded in rock and soil. Nor was any of this to be explained solely in terms of natural forces and the laws of nature; in these strange happenings a divine, miraculous force had been at work.

Scheuchzer became the leading proponent of what was to become an influential intellectual movement – the movement known to geologists and palaeontologists as diluvialism. As a contribution to the cause he produced, in 1708, a polemical pamphlet entitled *Piscium Querelae et Vindiciae* (*Complaints and Claims of the Fishes*). In excellent Latin the fish state their case:

> We, the swimmers, voiceless though we are, herewith lay our claim before the throne of Truth. We would reclaim what is rightly ours . . . Our claim is for the glory springing from the death of our ancestors . . . that race which lived and was carried on the waves before the Flood. . . . Moreover, we are defending an even greater cause: we bear irrefutable witness to the universal inundation.

In that cataclysm, the fish continue, fish and other marine creatures had to suffer, though they were wholly innocent: when the waters withdrew, they were left to perish on dry land. All this happened because of the sinfulness of human beings – and now human beings are degrading even the fossils, by refusing to recognize them for what they are: not the mineral offspring of stone but the remains of once-living creatures. A large fossil pike (present in illustration) is summoned to prove the justice of the claim, and does so by his very anatomy. Let unbelievers beware: their armour is shattered, their battle-lines are pierced, by the skill of this single pike, this authentic witness of the Flood.

The *Piscium Querelae* is a witty and eloquent tract which, apart from the fishes' complaint, contains engravings of fossilized skel-

30   Frontispiece detail from Scheuchzer's *Herbarium Diluvanium*, showing future fossils in the foreground.

etons of marine creatures, accompanied by careful descriptions. All in all, the work was well calculated both to explain the nature of animal fossils and to reaffirm the reality of the Flood. Unfortunately, Scheuchzer did not stop there. Years before, when a student at Altdorf, near Nuremberg, he had found a piece of shale with vertebrae embedded in it. A fragment with two vertebrae was still in his collection of fossils – and now, as he re-examined the fossil, he became convinced that these were human vertebrae. It was a small step to conclude that they came from a man who had drowned in the Flood – a member of the very generation whose sinfulness had caused the great calamity, and which had perished along with the guiltless fishes.

In the *Piscium Querelae* Scheuchzer published, along with the illustrations of fossil fishes, a drawing of the allegedly human vertebrae – and this gave rise to controversy. A former fellow student, Johann Baier, insisted that although these objects were undoubtedly genuine vertebrae, and no doubt came from a victim of the Flood, they had belonged not to a human being but to a fish. (In fact Scheuchzer and Baier were both mistaken: the vertebrae came from an ichthyosaur of the Jurassic period – but there was no way they could have conceived of that.)

Scheuchzer persisted. Near the western end of Lake Constance stood the village of Oeningen. From around 1500 limestone was quarried at Oeningen, and it was noticed, with astonishment, that images of countless plant-leaves, of totally unknown species, were imprinted on the strata. Fossils of fish, bullfrogs, snakes and turtles were also found in abundance. It is now known that these remains date from the Miocene epoch, some fifteen to twenty-five million years ago, when the area was covered with subtropical jungle, interspersed with shallow lakes; but to Scheuchzer, when he worked there early in the eighteenth century, all the fossils were obviously products of the Flood. That included an articulated skeleton, embedded in a stone slab, which came his way in 1725.

Just as he had misinterpreted the fossilized vertebrae in his collection, so he now misinterpreted this skeleton. What could it be but the skeleton of a man drowned in the Flood? He even gave the fossil a scientific name: *Homo diluvii testis*, 'Man who witnessed the Flood'. He sent descriptions of the fossil, in Latin, to Sir Hans Sloane, the President of the Royal Society, for publication in the Society's *Philosophical Transactions*; to the *Journal des Scavans*; and to German periodicals. He also published a book entitled *Homo diluvii testis*. It contains an engraving of the skeleton – and one is left wondering how anyone, let alone a physician, could have seen anything human in that strange object.

The gist of Scheuchzer's description is repeated in his *Physica Sacra* of 1731. It is as follows:

> It is certain that this schist is the half, or nearly so, of the skeleton of a man: that the substance even of the bones, and, what is more, of the flesh and of parts softer than the flesh, are there incorporated in the stone: in a word it is one of the rarest relics which we have of that cursed race which was buried under

31  'The man who witnessed the Flood'. From *Herbarium Diluvanium.*

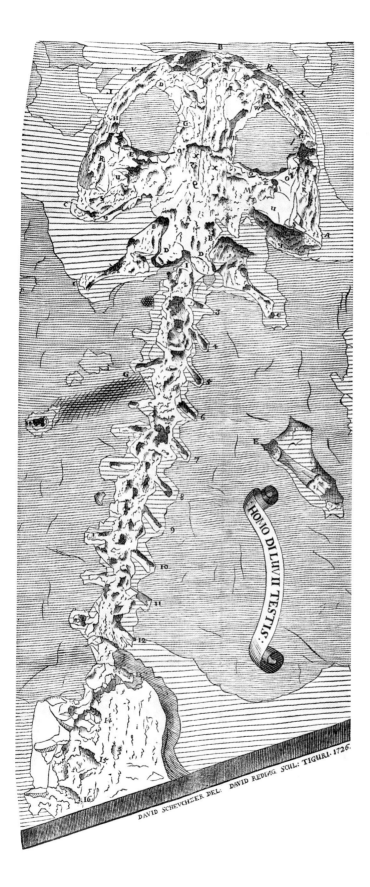

HOMO DILUVII TESTIS:

DAVID SCHEVCHZER DEL: DAVID REDING SCVL: TIGURI. 1726.

the waters. The figure shows us the contour of the frontal bone, the orbits with the openings which give passage to the great nerves of the fifth pair. We see there the remains of the brain, of the sphenoidal bone, of the roots of the nose, a notable fragment of the *os maxilla*, and some vestiges of the liver.[30]

Scheuchzer fully recognized that his find was almost without parallel, but he had an explanation for that:

> Up to the present, very few remains of human beings drowned in the Flood have been discovered. It may be that the reminders of blameless creatures such as plants, molluscs, fishes, even insects are more numerous because they deserved to be remembered better than the human beings – for all these latter, save for a few of Noah's relatives . . . richly deserved to be condemned to eternal oblivion.[31]

Scheuchzer's find caused a sensation. The skeleton was acquired by the Teyler Museum in Haarlem, and some sixty years were to pass before anyone doubted that it was indeed the skeleton of a witness and victim of the Flood. It was only in 1787 that the anatomist Petrus Camper detected Scheuchzer's error, and only in 1825 that the great palaeontologist Georges Cuvier examined the original 'witness of the Flood' – and at once recognized a giant salamander of the Miocene epoch.[32] Today the species still bears the name *Andrias scheuchzeri*.

Scheuchzer was a gifted scientist, perceptive, intuitive, restlessly enquiring; and his scientific achievements were considerable. He was the first to take measuring instruments into the Alps, the first in Switzerland to correlate barometric pressure with altitude, the first to tackle the problems presented by glaciers and by the sudden gales that sweep the mountains. He produced works containing descriptions and figures of great numbers of plants, minerals and fossils – works of lasting scientific value. He corresponded with leading philosophers and scientists all over Europe, and enjoyed international esteem. But he was also a notably devout man, whose last years were devoted to writing the four volumes of his *Physica Sacra*, in the hope of harmonizing Scripture and natural history once and for all. And it was of course that same hope that seduced him into his one colossal blunder.

Steno, Scheuchzer and especially Woodward had launched a vogue: it came to be taken for granted that fossils were the remains of living creatures which had perished in the Flood and had been carried by the Flood to their present placements. In England, above all, the notion figured in many works of local natural history: *The Natural History of Lancashire, Cheshire and the Peak in Derbyshire*, by the physician and naturalist Charles Leigh (1700), and *The Natural History of Northamptonshire*, by John Morton, rector of Oxenden and Fellow of the Royal Society (1712), are two of the best.

However, this view of fossils and their origin soon became hard to sustain. For by the middle of the eighteenth century the biblical time-scale itself was being called in question – with the result that beliefs about the Flood were changing yet again.

# Chapter 8

## *Shifting Time-Scales*

1

Though the scientific revolution of the sixteenth and seventeenth centuries had shattered the traditional view of space, it left the traditional view of time intact. The earth was no longer at the centre of the universe, its surrounding crystalline spheres were dissolved, the move (to borrow a famous phrase) 'from the closed world to the infinite universe' was under way – and still, mainly on the basis of the genealogies in Genesis, the age of the earth was fixed at around six thousand years.

The Christian apologist Theophilus of Antioch had offered such a computation as early as the second century.[1] Medieval theologians accepted it, the Protestant scholars of the Reformation not only adhered to it but insisted on it. Commonly dismissed nowadays as ludicrous, it emerges as eminently reasonable when set in its historical context. At a time when neither fossils nor stratification were yet fully understood, the only sources for earth-history were written records. Anyone who intended to trace the history of mankind back to its beginnings needed to be conversant not only with the Old Testament in its various versions but also with classical and oriental languages, with ancient history, with astronomy, with calendrical lore, above all with the techniques of textual and historical criticism. Then he would be qualified to collate the biblical genealogies and stories with other ancient documentary sources. And in arriving at the origin of mankind he would of necessity arrive also at the origin of the earth – for few doubted that mankind and the earth were coeval, born of a single divine act of creation.

Historical chronology was a highly respected form of scholarship, and formidable scholars devoted themselves to it.[2] The *Opus de Emendatione Temporum* of the Protestant Joseph Justus Scaliger (1583) and the *Opus de Doctrina Temporum* of the Jesuit Dionysius Patavius (1627) were established authorities long before the most celebrated practitioner of all, James Ussher (or Usher), Archbishop of Armagh and Primate of All Ireland, tried his hand.

Ussher (1581–1656) was not only an eminent churchman, he played an important part in affairs of state, as Privy Councillor and a confidant of Charles I. Despite this connection, such was his prestige that at his death in 1656 Cromwell himself ordered that he be given a public funeral and burial in Westminster Abbey, with full honours. And Ussher also had an international reputation as a brilliant and versatile scholar. No fanatic or eccentric, untouched by what in his day was called 'enthusiasm', he applied a trained, learned and cautious mind to the Bible story – and if he was mistaken in treating it as a totally reliable source, so were almost all his contemporaries.

Ussher's great work was published in two parts, *Annales Veteris Testamenti* and *Annalium Pars Posterior*, in 1650 and 1654 respectively; an English translation followed in 1658. The author's standing and repute ensured that the work would be taken as supremely reliable, almost as though it had the authority of Scripture itself. Indeed, in 1701 the chronology based on this work was inserted into the margin of a new edition of the Authorised Version – with the result that it came to be known as 'The Received Chronology', even 'The Bible Chronology'.

Nothing in Ussher's work was more convincing than its opening pages, for they were based on Genesis – and, as everyone knew, Genesis had been composed by God himself and dictated by him to 'the greatest Natural Philosopher that ever lived upon this Earth', Moses.[3] Ussher supplied precise times both for the Creation and for the Flood. Heaven and earth were created on the evening preceding Sunday 23 October 4004 BCE; and it was on that Sunday that

God, together with the highest Heaven, created the Angels. Then, having finished, as it were, the roofe of this building, he fell in hand with the foundation of this wonderful Fabrick of the World, he fashioned this lowermost Globe, consisting of the Deep, and of the Earth; all the Quire of Angels singing together, and magnifying his name therefore.

As for the Flood, that occurred 1,656 years after the Creation. The day on which Noah and his family joined the animals in the ark was Sunday 7 December 2349 BCE. The day on which the ark came to rest on Mount Ararat was 6 May in the following year. On Thursday 18 December Noah and his family came out of the ark, 'and God restored the nature of things destroyed by the flood'.[4]

Ussher's computations reinforced the generally accepted view: not only the general public but scholars and scientists took it for granted that the estimate of about six thousand years was correct. And that remained the case long after Ussher's time. In a book review in the *Philosophical Transactions* of the Royal Society for 1730, for instance, all chronologies which suggested that Chinese civilization was older than that were summarily rejected. 'Such Chimeras', wrote the critic, 'deserve not the Pain of refuting. They are equally repugnant to good Sense, the Rules of Criticism, and to Religion.'[5]

2

Such an exiguous time-scale ensured that the Flood would keep all its importance. As scientific curiosity spread abroad, the peculiarities of the earth's surface attracted ever more attention. It was inconceivable that the earth should have had a rugged, disjointed appearance when God first created it – yet six thousand years seemed too short a time for slow, cumulative change to have had such an effect: some catastrophe or catastrophes must be responsible.

The Flood provided the most obvious explanation. Every perplexing feature of the earth's surface, from continents and ocean basins down to hillocks and caves, was ascribed to that unique, overwhelming disaster. So Thomas Burnet had concluded already in the 1670s – but Burnet was no geologist. If some who are counted, rightly, amongst the pioneers of modern, scientific geology were still holding to that view in the second half of the eighteenth century, that was because the biblical time-scale left them no option.

To appreciate just how difficult it was to discard an assumption which was both so venerable and so universally accepted one need only glance at the writings of two reputable geologists, one English, the other German. Alexander Catcott (1725–79) was a Bristol clergyman and schoolmaster who carried out geological fieldwork in the surrounding countryside. His *Treatise on the Deluge*, first published in 1761 and again, in a much enlarged version, in 1768, shows a typical mixture of careful observation, intelligent questioning and mistaken conclusions.[6]

Working in the Mendip Hills, Catcott was impressed both by the evidence of stratification and by the discontinuous distribution of the strata. The present condition of the land reminded him of a ruined building:

> . . . if a person was to see the broken walls of a palace or castle that had been in part demolished, he would certainly conclude that the breaches or vacant spaces in those walls were once filled with similar substances, and in conjunction with the rest of the walls, could easily with his eye see the lines in which the walls were carried, and in thought fill up the breaches and re-unite the whole: And in the same manner if a person was to view the naked ends or broken edges of the strata in a mountain on one side of the valley and compare them with their corre-sponding ends in the mountain on the other side of the valley, he would manifestly perceive that the space between each was once filled up, and the strata continued from mountain to mountain.[7]

What could have caused such changes? Earthquakes, Catcott rightly decided, could not provide an adequate explanation – but in that case, what could, if not flowing water? The six-thousand-year limit prevented Catcott from invoking, as a present-day geologist might, gradual erosion by fluvial action. The only possi-bility, it seemed, was swift erosion by the waters of the Flood. Fortunately, the Flood was an established fact, Moses' account being 'philosophically just and literally true: and . . . strictly consistent with nature'.[8]

Catcott's explanation of how the Flood came about is as extravagant as anything proposed by Burnet or Whiston.[9] In the beginning, he maintains, the earth had air at its centre and was also surrounded by air and light. The earth's surface was a spherical crust, with a layer of water on its inner and outer surfaces, both layers being held in place by the pressure of the air. Unfortunately, light from the sun leaked through the crust, causing the inner air to expand until it cracked the crust. Part of the outer waters rushed through the cracks and combined with the inner waters, expelling the air inside the earth. As they rushed downwards the waters furrowed the land and made mountains and valleys on what had hitherto been a perfect sphere. Now the earth's centre consisted solely of water – the great abyss of Scripture.[10] When God decided to produce the Flood he needed only to increase the air pressure on the seas until they too poured into the abyss, then to increase it still further until all the water inside the earth was forced upwards to flood the globe. The pressure of the waters as they were pushed upwards cracked the earth's crust a second time.[11]

What Catcott has to tell of the course and effects of the Flood is clearly influenced by Woodward's famous *Essay*. All metals and minerals, he explains, were dissolved by the Flood, but organic matter, being light and held together by its fibres, remained whole. God having, at the appropriate time, changed the atmospheric pressure yet again, everything – the atomized minerals and metals, the intact vegetables and animal remains and seeds – settled back into almost the same places as they had occupied before the Flood. A new earth emerged – but this new earth differed from the former earth in some respects. It bore the remains of once-living creatures stranded and fossilized on the mountains, to remind human beings of the Flood. Also, it had those irregular strata which had launched Catcott on his enquiry; these, he decided, were produced by upward pressure of the air, which impeded a smooth subsidence of matter after the Flood.[12]

Johann Gottlob Lehmann (1719–67) was a much greater scientist than Catcott. His interests included medicine, chemistry, mineralogy and mining as well as geology; and as a geologist he was

outstanding.[13] On the strength of his own careful observations in
the mountains of central Germany, he produced a classification
of mountains which has remained valuable. The book in which
he summarized his findings was published in 1756 – and in that
standard work, Geikie's *Founders of Geology*, published in 1906, it is
still recognized as a classical monograph. But Lehmann's account
of how the various kinds of mountain came into existence is
interesting for quite a different reason: just like Catcott's book, it
shows how a geologist who unquestioningly accepted the biblical
time-scale was compelled to invoke Genesis, and particularly the
story of the Flood, to make sense of his own observations.

Lehmann classified mountains according to their position,
structure and mineral content. There were primeval mountains,
which underlay and also overtopped all younger mountains.
Scripture showed that these mountains were as old as the earth
itself. The biblical account of Creation suggested, in general
terms, how they had taken shape in the depths of the ocean,
before life existed on earth; that accounted for the fact that they
contained no organic remains. On the other hand, there were
biblical references to the art of mining, which suggested that the
primitive earth had already had its ore-bearing mountains – and
sure enough, these primeval mountains still abounded in metals.

During the Flood the waters had covered even the highest
mountains, sweeping them clean of all loose material – which was
why the primeval mountains were now bare. Eventually the earthy
material was deposited, layer upon layer, in nearby plains and
valleys. This was the origin of secondary, or stratified, mountains
– and it also accounted for the presence in such mountains of the
remains and impressions of fishes, crabs, plants and flowers.
There were also mountains of a third kind, which had come into
being only after the Flood; these had been formed by the action
of earthquakes, volcanic eruptions, local inundations and other
accidents of nature. But Lehmann's main interest was in how the
secondary mountains came into being and how the primeval
mountains acquired their present form. The Flood, he insisted,
was responsible for all this, and more: it had even changed the
interior of the earth, creating caverns, holes and hollow passages
where none had been before.[14]

Catcott and Lehmann were by no means alone in trying to

harmonize the ever-increasing geological and palaeontological data with the biblical time-scale. But meanwhile notions about the age of the earth were being drastically revised.

## 3

The process by which the perceived age of the earth grew from some six thousand years to some four and a half billion has been abundantly studied.[15] What matters here is that already in its early stages, in the late eighteenth and early nineteenth centuries, the expansion of the time-scale called in question the role that traditionally had been ascribed to the Flood.

There had been a curious prelude. In England – perhaps because ecclesiastical censorship was less rigorous there than in most countries on the Continent – the biblical time-scale was questioned, briefly and hesitantly, in the years 1693–95.

In 1693 a Fellow of the Royal Society, John Beaumont, produced *Considerations on a Book, Entituled The Theory of the Earth* – and it is quite clear from that critique of Burnet that he would have liked to repudiate the pentateuchal chronology altogether. In the event, he merely notes some of the problems raised by that chronology, and adds that if it were permissible to deviate from the 'Mosaic' account, he would choose to regard the earth as eternal, or at least as so old that its origins are for ever lost to human knowledge. One may suspect that similar thoughts were often hazarded in London coffee-houses.

Scientists had their own reasons for doubt. In 1695 John Ray, generally regarded as the greatest naturalist of his time, wrote to his friend Edward Lhwyd, the Keeper of the Ashmolean Museum, Oxford, on the subject of fossils. He accepted that these strange objects were of organic origin, but was uneasy about the implications: 'there follows such a train of consequences, as seem to shock the Scripture-History of the novity of the World.'[16] For his part Lhwyd, though sceptical about the significance of fossils, was led to a similar conclusion by considering the thousands of boulders which had rolled down from the mountains into the valleys in his native Wales. They fell so seldom, he wrote to Ray, that such an accumulation must have required 'many thousands of Years more than the Age of the World'.[17]

These were tentative reflections, but – as we have seen[18] – the second of the papers which Edmund Halley read to the Royal Society went much further. If, before there were any human beings at all, the earth really underwent many catastrophes, each of which destroyed whatever kind of life was in existence at the time to make way for a new kind – then the earth must be very old indeed, and the biblical Flood is reduced to one episode among many. That thought too was uttered in 1694 – even though, for fear of incurring 'the Censure of the Sacred Order', its publication was delayed for some thirty years.

It was almost a century later, and chiefly in France, that the age of the earth became a matter of public and sustained debate. From around 1770 onwards the six-thousand-year scheme began to be reinterpreted. Educated people noted that Moses had written the account of the Creation for the benefit of the uneducated; so it was quite in order to interpret it allegorically, with each day of the six days converted into an epoch of indeterminate but vast duration. Moreover, those epochs could be seen as making up the history of the earth before the appearance of mankind. The seventh day could be allotted to human history – and there the traditional time-scale might well be valid: there was after all no reason, at that time, to think that mankind had existed for more than six thousand years or so.

Buffon's famous *Époques de la nature* (1778) shows how such a reinterpretation could affect ideas about the Flood. On the strength of much research and experiment Buffon announced that the earth had existed for 74,832 years; his private estimates, as the manuscript shows, were revised upwards from 3,000,000 to 10,000,000.[19] Mankind, however, had emerged only some six to eight thousand years ago, somewhere in Central Asia. And the lot of those early human beings was utterly wretched. Naked in mind and body, defenceless against the elements, they underwent calamities which left an indelible mark on human consciousness. These included local inundations, which were transformed in memory into a universal catastrophe.[20] Not that there were no universal deluges – only, the last of these had occurred some 35,000 years before mankind came into existence. Set in such a context, the biblical Flood was reduced to the status of a minor episode, a mishap too commonplace to be singled out for special mention.

In the writings of the Scottish geologist James Hutton (1726–97) the Flood fares even worse. In histories of science Hutton is often spoken of as one of the founders of historical geology, but his greatest achievement was to have perceived in mere stones the proof of the unimaginable antiquity of the earth.[21] In his *Theory of the Earth* he aimed to demonstrate in the earth's history the same unchanging order as Newton had discovered in the heavens. The earth is portrayed as a self-regulating, self-renewing machine, whose laws of operation are as unchanging as those followed by the heavenly bodies. Dynamic forces in the earth's crust create tensions which, in course of time, bring the ocean-bed to the surface, while land-masses are eroded and sink under the waters: so the earth is always decaying and always renewing itself. The book closes with the famous phrase, 'we find no vestige of a beginning – no prospect of an end'. Make of those words what one will, this much is clear: illimitable vistas of time are opened up. It is equally clear that no place at all is left for the Flood. Hutton himself recognized as much – the buried shell-beds are explained as legacies not of the Flood but of subsidence and renewed uplift.

Hutton read his *Theory of the Earth* to the Royal Society of Edinburgh in 1785, and it was published in the Society's *Proceedings* three years later. An amplified two-volume edition was issued in 1795. The dismay with which it was greeted was largely due to the political situation. Many Britons had been profoundly shocked by the excesses of the revolutionary era in France, and were convinced that these horrors were due to the spread of deism, scepticism and atheism. By arguing for the immense age, if not the eternity, of the earth, Hutton seemed to be aligning himself with those foreign miscreants – and the fact that in reality he was a pious man of conservative views did not save him from condemnation.

Was that all? It has been said that neither the sun nor death can be looked at steadily. The same could be said of 'the dark abyss of time'.[22] Two centuries ago nobody, of course, had the faintest inkling of how unimaginably deep that abyss would prove to be. Nobody could have conceived of the facts to which we have had to accommodate ourselves: that our species has existed only for a tiny moment in the thousands of millions of years that make up

32   James Hutton, by Sir Henry Raeburn.

the history of the earth; and that countless other species survived hundreds of times longer, only to vanish in the end. Still, one may feel some sympathy with those contemporaries of Buffon and of Hutton who, when the time-scale began to shift, averted their gaze.

   A great disorientation threatened, a terrifying loss of emotional security. To many it seemed imperative that the authority of revealed religion be reasserted. The Flood acquired fresh importance: against Buffon and against Hutton, it must be shown to have been the unique manifestation of divine omnipotence described in Genesis.

## 4

The rehabilitation of the Flood was undertaken, with enthusiasm, by the Irishman Richard Kirwan (1733–1812).[23]

Kirwan was a polymath: his published work ranges from meteorology to music, from philology to philosophy. Resident in London from 1769 to 1782, he was elected Fellow of the Royal Society and even received the Society's Copley medal; and by the time he returned to Dublin, he had an international reputation as a scientist. Every kind of honour came his way: he was one of the first honorary members of the newly founded Geological Society of London, corresponding member of other learned societies throughout Europe, President of the Royal Irish Academy, and Inspector General of His Majesty's Mines in Ireland. It was left for later generations to realize how little he added to the sum of geological knowledge.

In Dublin Kirwan was noted for his kindness and generosity and indifference to money – and also for his eccentricities. In addition to two Irish wolfhounds, two mastiffs and two greyhounds, all outsize, he kept an eagle, which perched on his shoulder when he walked or rode. Much concerned not to catch cold, he wore a 'large-leafed hat flapped low over his face' even indoors – which effectively prevented him from attending church. And when, at the age of 79, he did catch a cold, he tried to cure it by starving it – and ended by starving himself to death.

Kirwan's writings were as colourful as his personality. In a paper which he presented to the Royal Irish Academy in 1793, and more amply in his *Geological Essays* of 1799, he attacked Hutton in the language not of science but of religious dogmatism. The function of geology, he insisted, 'graduates into religion, as this does into morality'.[24] As recent experience had shown, to impugn the account which Genesis gave of the Creation 'has proved too favourable to the structure of various systems of atheism or infidelity, as these have been in their turn to turbulence and immorality'.[25] By insisting on the antiquity of the earth Hutton was undermining the very basis of society; Kirwan was appalled to note 'how fatal the suspicion of the high antiquity of the globe has been to the credit of Mosaic history, and consequently to religion and morality'.[26] Hutton had shown himself to be an atheist, no

33　*The Deluge, Toward its Close*, by Joshua Shaw, *c.* 1804.

less. Fortunately his arguments were so absurd that Kirwan had found it unnecessary to read his book through.[27]

Intemperate and misguided though Kirwan's onslaught was, it had some positive results. It was in response to Kirwan's paper of 1793 that Hutton prepared the fullest statement of his ideas, in the amplified version of his *Theory of the Earth.* And it was in response to that work that Kirwan in turn produced the fullest statement of his own geological ideas – which, though scientifically valueless, include wonderfully imaginative speculations about the Flood.

Kirwan's *Geological Essays* deal with both the Creation and the Flood. The earth, we are told, was formed by precipitation from a primordial 'chaotic fluid'. For some centuries while the crust was solidifying the fluid continued to cover it, but gradually the level sank, to form the present oceans, leaving the present continents dry. Then came the Flood.

The Flood originated in 'the greatest collection of waters on the face of the globe'[28] – the southern ocean, extending from India and South America to the South Pole. That explained an otherwise incomprehensible fact. Fossilized remains of tropical animals and plants and shells had recently been discovered as far north as Siberia.[29] Obviously they had been carried there by the Flood; indeed, 'as the elephants very naturally crowded together on the approach of the inundation, they were conveyed in flocks, and hence their bones are found in accumulated heaps, as should be expected'.[30]

As it swept northwards with 'resistless impetuosity' the Flood reshaped some continents and shattered others. Once there had been a land-mass in the north Pacific, uniting Asia and America: that was almost annihilated, so that only a few islands remain. Then the Flood swept across Asia and North America, in some places dashing mountains to pieces, in others reducing the land to barren deserts such as the Gobi. Further south in the Pacific another branch of the Flood poured out to excavate the Gulfs to Tonkin and Siam, the Bay of Bengal, the Arabian, Red and Caspian Seas, and to transform Persia, Arabia and North Africa to sandy waste. Yet another branch of the Flood swept northwards up the Atlantic until, somewhere to the west of Ireland, it met the torrent which had come across land from the Pacific. 'The effect of the encounter of such enormous masses of water, rushing in opposite directions, must have been stupendous, it was such as appears to have shaken and shattered some of the solid vaults that supported the subjacent strata of the globe.'[31] Now the land-mass joining Central and South America with Africa was submerged, to form the bed of the Atlantic Ocean. Incidental consequences included the steep and rugged western coasts of Ireland, Scotland and Norway and of many of the islands in the West Indies.

Much of the earth's crust remained so unstable that a series of earthquakes ensued. These continued until around 2000 BCE, producing the Irish Sea, the Straits of Dover and Gibraltar, the Dardanelles, the Kattegat, the Bering Straits. Moreover, like so many before him, Kirwan was convinced that the Flood also had disastrous long-term effects, which are with us still. The putrefying animals and fish absorbed so much oxygen that the atmosphere has been impoverished ever since: 'Hence the constitution of men must have been weakened and the lives of their enfeebled posterity greatly reduced to their present standard.'

In his dogmatic rejection of the antiquity of the earth, in his insistence that any such notion must necessarily undermine not only religion but society and even morality, Kirwan was a pioneer of fundamentalism. He was to have many successors in the nineteenth and twentieth centuries. And for them the Genesis story of the Flood would be what it was for him: at once a central article of faith and a subject of endless elaboration.

34   *The Deluge*, by John Martin, 1834. At the time when the debate about the historicity of the Flood was at its height, the story appealed as strongly as ever to the Romantic imagination.

# Chapter 9

## *Harmonizers*

1

Was Kirwan's the only way of rehabilitating the Flood? Or could one, while holding fast to the historicity and, more, the unique importance of the Flood, also accept the antiquity of the earth? In the same year as Kirwan presented his paper to the Royal Irish Academy, 1793, a Swiss called Jean-André de Luc published, in the *British Critic* of London, his 'Geological Letters to Professor Blumenbach'. When it was republished as a book the work carried the title *Letters on the Physical History of the Earth, containing Geological and Historical Proofs of the Divine Mission of Moses*, and this is a fair description. De Luc had ventured on an attempt – perhaps the earliest – to harmonize Genesis with the findings of geology concerning the age of the earth.

De Luc (1727–1817) was a serious geologist.[1] He travelled widely not only in the Alps but also in France, Germany, the Netherlands and England, struggling over trackless countrysides, up mountain peaks and down mines, climbing towers and church spires. For some sixty-five years he accumulated geological data and built up a fine museum of natural history in general and of mineralogy in particular. He knew a great deal about the present state of the earth, and his major works are largely devoted to detailed descriptions of its strata. In his works he was careful to summarize and discuss the ideas of his predecessors and contemporaries before giving his own. He was invariably courteous to his critics and opponents, and he had an enviable international reputation as a scientist.

De Luc defined his aim with admirable clarity. Looking back on the fifty years that he had spent in geological investigations he felt that they had been well spent, for they had 'demonstrated the conformity of geological monuments with the sublime account of that series of operations which took place during the Six Days, as periods of time, recorded by the inspired penman'. The penman Moses knew no physics or geology, nor did Noah; yet Genesis was a perfect description of what modern geology shows to have happened. Only divine revelation could account for that.[2]

This was true not only of the Creation but also of the Flood. De Luc was convinced that there had been a universal deluge at the time assigned to it in Genesis, and that the earth owed its present form to that catastrophe; and his chief aim was to demonstrate, from observable phenomena, that such was indeed the case. On the other hand, he was certain that the six 'days' of Genesis were meant to be understood allegorically: really they were epochs of indeterminate length. The earth's strata revealed the characteristics of each of the six epochs. The fifth epoch saw the emergence of the first animals, in the sixth epoch human beings existed alongside animals. The Flood marked the end of the sixth period.

Up to that point the continents were different from ours, and much larger. The cause of the Flood was a slow infiltration of liquid under the crust of those ancient continents. Under the sea-bed volcanic eruptions had gradually produced enormous caverns. Now a sudden rush of liquid into these caverns caused them to collapse, and with them all the continents resting on them. When all human beings were drowned, their bones sank to the bottom of the sea, so it was not surprising that no human fossils had been found.

As the continents subsided the sea rushed into the gap, leaving its original bed; and the former sea-bed became our modern continents. Some islands in the ancient sea were not submerged, and these became our mountain peaks. Animals living on those islands were also saved from the Flood. They migrated down the slopes, joined up with the animals saved in the ark and, together with them, repopulated the earth. And if little of all this was to be found in Genesis, that was because Moses portrayed only that part of the Flood which Noah had witnessed.

The new earth was very different from the old. The earth's centre of gravity was altered, which affected both its rotary motion and the inclination of its axis. Inevitably the atmosphere too was modified, so that outside the torrid zone great variations in temperature obtained, between summer and winter, day and night. And these changes in turn affected the earth's inhabitants: some species died out, the human life span was drastically reduced.[3]

So though the biblical time-scale is no longer taken literally – is in effect abandoned – the Flood retains all its significance. Viewed as a relatively recent event in an immensely long history of the earth, it still looms as a unique, and uniquely important, event. If such an attitude had little appeal in revolutionary or post-revolutionary France, where intellectual life was deeply influenced by the Enlightenment, it had a great appeal in conservative England – which no doubt is why de Luc chose to spend the last half of his ninety years in England, and why he flourished there, as a Fellow of the Royal Society and Reader to Queen Charlotte, comfortably housed at Windsor when not on his travels – which also seem to have been financed by the queen.

2

In England writings by de Luc continued to appear, and to be taken seriously, for many years – an *Elementary Treatise on Geology* in 1809, a new edition of the *Letters on the Physical History of the Earth*, posthumously, as late as 1831. Meanwhile his argument about the Flood was thought – albeit mistakenly – to have found support in the work of a far greater scientist, the Swiss/French anatomist and paleontologist Georges Cuvier (1769–1832). In his *Recherches sur les ossemens fossiles* (1812) Cuvier showed how the forms of dinosaurs and flying reptiles could be reconstructed from fragmentary, fossilized relics; and that massive work sold steadily for thirty years and more. Most influential of all was the book's preface, in which Cuvier expounded his notions about earth-history. This was at once recognized as a work of outstanding importance. Issued separately, under the title *Discours sur les révolutions de la surface du globe*, it went through far more editions than the parent work, was widely translated, and had much influence among the general reading public as well as among scientists and scholars. The English translation, by Robert Jameson, with the (so familiar!) title *Essay on the Theory of the Earth*, had four editions between 1817 and 1827.

What the *Discours* offers is a coherently organized and attractively written summary of ideas which the author had long entertained and advocated. Cuvier argues that down the ages conditions on earth were generally as tranquil as they are today – but were nevertheless transformed from time to time by sudden global catastrophes. The major changes, or 'revolutions', in physical geography which then took place were so radical that they extinguished many animal species – which explains why fossil remains include many species which are not now to be found anywhere in the world. The notion was not new; but Cuvier gave it a scientific basis such as it had not possessed before. With the help of the new science of comparative anatomy (of which he was in effect the inventor) he was able to show that, with each revolution, the living things inhabiting the earth had indeed changed, some species disappearing, others coming into being; so the number and order of the revolutions could be determined.

Cuvier mistakenly concluded that one such revolution must have taken place quite recently, and abruptly. What he has to say about it is summarized in a paragraph of the *Discours*:

> If there is any circumstance thoroughly established in geology, it is, that the crust of our globe has been subjected to a great and sudden revolution, the epoch of which cannot be dated much further back than five or six thousand years ago; and that this revolution had buried all the countries which were before inhabited by men and by the other animals now best known ... that the small number of individuals of men and other animals that escaped from the effects of that great revolution have since propagated and spread over the lands then newly laid dry; and consequently that the human race has only resumed a progressive state of improvement since that epoch, by forming established societies, raising monuments, collecting natural facts, and constructing systems of science and learning.[4]

Cuvier was happy to assume that that revolution was the same as the Flood recorded in Genesis and in other ancient documents –

but he did not stress the point. Nor did he ever suggest that any of the revolutions undergone by the earth had a supernatural cause. Though a prominent member of the French Protestant community he was also a man of the Enlightenment; and he always maintained that science and religion should be kept strictly separate. However, in the preface which Jameson gave to his translation of the *Discours* the Flood figures as a supernatural event; and that helped to determine the interpretation that English scientists imposed on Cuvier's insights.

The time was ripe. Just at the time when Cuvier's book was circulating in England, field investigations were unearthing what looked like traces of a relatively recent cataclysm. How else was one to explain the great erratic boulders strewn over much of Europe and North America, often high in the mountains and far from their place of origin? Or the mantle of boulder clay and shelly and bedded drift which was so widespread in the northern hemisphere? As we now know, there was in fact another and better explanation; but at that time nobody was aware that ice-sheets had once covered most of Europe and North America. Given the lack of a glacial theory, it is no wonder that the educated public looked to the Flood. And in the English context that meant looking to Genesis.

This was especially true of the distinctively English school of historical geology, or earth-history, which was just coming into being.[5] This school originated at Oxford and its most formidable protagonist, William Buckland (1784–1856), was Oxford's first Reader, and subsequently Professor, of Geology. As it developed the school came to include prominent Cambridge figures such as Adam Sedgwick and William Whewell. All these men had taken holy orders (Buckland was to end his days as Dean of Westminster), and many of the students to whom they lectured were destined for the Church. At that time the ancient universities of England were barely touched by the secular philosophies of history which were flourishing on the Continent: scientific enquiry was expected to be carried on within a context of religious orthodoxy. If it was to be accepted as a legitimate academic subject, historical geology had to adjust itself to that ancient Anglican tradition.

Buckland was a flamboyant character, as celebrated for his

35  *Right*: William Buckland,
by Thomas Phillips.

36  *Facing page*: Buckland
lecturing to senior members
of Oxford University.

eccentricities as for his teaching. It was his boast that he had eaten
his way through the entire animal kingdom; and exaggerated
though the claim was, it reflected his ambition well enough. A
childhood friend of Buckland's sons has recorded his recollection
of the great man's rooms in Christ Church:

> I recall . . . the side table in the dining room covered with fos-
> sils, 'paws off' in large letters on a protecting card; the very
> sideboard candlesticks perched on saurian vertebrae; the queer
> dishes garnishing the dinner table – horseflesh I remembered
> more than once, crocodile another day, mice baked in batter
> on a third day – while the guinea pig under the table inquir-
> ingly nibbled at your infantine toes, the bear walked round your
> chair and rasped your hand with file-like tongue, the jackal's
> fiendish yell close by came through the open window . . .

That jackal might make one wonder: childhood fantasies rather than true recollections? But probably one would be wrong, for it is known that Buckland really did keep a hyena. Which makes it easier to believe another tale of eccentricity from the same source:

Frank (Buckland's son) used to tell of their visit . . . to a foreign cathedral where was exhibited a martyr's blood – dark spots on the pavement ever fresh and ineradicable. The professor dropped on the pavement and touched the stain with his tongue. 'I can tell you what it is; it is bat's urine.'[6]

Buckland's eccentricities extended to his manner of teaching. When he sent his students on a field excursion he would meet them, in a cavern or on a mud bank, clad in academic gown and top hat. When he lectured – at first in the Old Ashmolean Museum, later in the Clarendon Building – it was against a background of jumbled rocks, skulls and skeletons. The lectures themselves were no less eccentric – but they were also excellent: they attracted large audiences, and held professors as well as undergraduates spellbound.

Buckland's teaching centred on the Flood, and very effectively too. At a time when it was already largely discredited on the Continent, diluvial geology flourished so vigorously at Oxford that the 1820s have been called 'the diluvial decade'. In his inaugural lecture of 1819 (published the following year under the title *Vindiciae Geologicae; or the Connexion of Geology with Religion Explained*) Buckland summarized the evidence for the Flood as a decisive event in earth-history:

> Again, the grand fact of *an universal deluge* at no very remote period is proved on grounds so decisive and incontrovertible, that, had we never heard of such an event from Scripture, or any other authority, Geology of itself must have called in the assistance of some such catastrophe, to explain the phenomena of diluvian action which are universally presented to us, and which are unintelligible without recourse to a deluge exerting its ravages at a period not more ancient than that announced in the Book of Genesis.[7]

Like de Luc, Buckland set the Flood in a long temporal per-spective. The six days of Genesis were not to be taken literally. Between each of God's acts of creation and the next, thousands of ages might well have supervened; tens of thousands of ages might have preceded the Flood. Since these epochs had no bearing on mankind, Moses had of course disregarded them. By contrast the Flood, as 'the last great change that has affected the surface of the earth',[8] had profoundly modified the conditions of human life.

In his *Reliquiae Diluvianae; or, Observations on . . . Geological Phen-omena, Attesting the Action of an Universal Deluge* (1823–4) Buckland described what the Flood had achieved. He did not believe that tropical fossils found in Europe had been brought there by the Flood, over a distance of thousands of miles. On the contrary, when confronted with a mass of hyena bones in the Kirkdale Cave in Yorkshire, he rightly decided that there must have been a change of climate in the northern hemisphere.[9] But there, he argued, the Flood must indeed have played a part: though a recent and transient inundation, it had been powerful enough to change the climate.

The Flood had done more than that. As a direct agent of divine power the Flood not only practically annihilated mankind and all animal species, it also devastated the earth, tearing up its solid strata and reducing its surface to a state of ruin. Unsorted deposits of clay and gravel, huge boulders scattered across hills and valleys, the very shape of hills and valleys, were all interpreted as legacies of the Flood.[10]

These were powerful statements, and for some years they were very widely accepted as true. During the 1820s the reviews gave more attention to natural history than to all the other sciences put together – and reviews as diverse as the relatively free-thinking *Edinburgh Review* and the devout *Quarterly Review* were at one in commending Buckland and the *Reliquiae Diluvianae*. The Flood seemed firmly established as the latest of the great cataclysms, but also as a supernatural event – a uniquely important happening linking the sacred records with the doctrine of global revolutions, and illustrating the concordance of Genesis and geology. In 1825 Buckland's most illustrious disciple, the Woodwardian Professor of Geology at Cambridge, Adam Sedgwick, produced an admirable summary of the current assumption:

> The sacred records tell us – that a few thousand years ago 'the foundations of the great deep' were broken up – and that the earth's surface was submerged by the water of a general deluge; and the investigations of geology tend to prove that the accumulations of alluvial matter have not been going on many thousands of years; and that they were preceded by a great catastrophe which has left traces of its operation in the diluvial detritus which is spread out over all the strata of the world.
>
> Between these conclusions, derived from sources entirely independent of each other, there is, therefore, a general coincidence which it would be most unreasonable to deny.[11]

## 3

Not everyone was impressed by these attempts to force Genesis into agreement with the latest developments in earth-science.

What grounds were there, after all, for assuming that the Flood had been violent enough to modify the surface of the earth? In 1826, when Buckland's prestige was at its height, the Presbyterian minister John Fleming pointed out that whereas Buckland spoke of a sudden and violent flood which left its mark on every valley and gorge, Moses had spoken of water rising gently for forty days, and leaving no lasting trace except the rainbow.[12] Fleming was not only a minister, he was also a prominent member of Edinburgh's leading natural history society and the author of a book entitled *Philosophy of Geology; or, A General View of the Structure, Functions and Classification of Animals*. Nor did he stand alone amongst scientists. Before long the great Charles Lyell was saying much the same. In his epoch-making *Principles of Geology* he declared 'that the earth's surface underwent no great modification in the era of the Mosaic deluge, and that the scriptural narrative does not warrant us in expecting to find any geological monuments of the catastrophe'.[13] No doubt with tongue in cheek, Lyell even repeated an ancient argument: the olive-leaf which the dove brought to Noah as a sign that the waters were retiring must have come from a tree that was still standing – and how could a deluge which was unable to uproot an olive-tree have thrown up lofty mountains or turned the sea-bed into dry land?[14]

Buckland himself was more affected by another, very different consideration: the fact that no human fossils had been found in supposedly diluvial deposits. An open-minded man with a scientist's respect for evidence, Buckland was disturbed by that hiatus. Granted, de Luc had argued that, since land and sea had changed places, all human fossils must necessarily be at the bottom of the sea; but Buckland was not persuaded that any such interchange had taken place. Reluctantly, he came round to the view that the last geological deluge must indeed have taken place in very remote times, before there were any human beings.

As Buckland abandoned the diluvial theory, so did his followers. Adam Sedgwick spoke for many in his last address as President of the Geological Society in 1831:

Having been myself a believer, and, to the best of my power, a propagator of what I now regard as a philosophic heresy . . . I think it right, as one of my last acts before I quit this Chair, thus publicly to read my recantation.

We ought, indeed, to have paused before we first adopted the diluvian theory, and referred all our old superficial gravel to the action of the Mosaic Flood. For of man, and the works of his hands, we have not yet found a single trace among the remnants of a former world entombed in these deposits.[15]

Buckland made no such dramatic disavowal; but in *Geology and Mineralogy Considered with Reference to Natural Theology* (begun in 1832 though published only in 1836, in the series known as the *Bridgewater Treatises*) he quietly disentangled the history of mankind from earth-history. The identification of the six days of Creation with periods of geological time was abandoned, and there was no longer any pretence that the Flood could be connected with geology. And when, in 1840, the Swiss Louis Agassiz propounded his glacial theory to the Geological Society in London, Buckland's diluvial theory came to be seen as what it was: one of the many imaginative but mistaken ventures that have accompanied the development of earth-science.

37    *The Eve of the Deluge,* by John Linnell, *c.* 1880.

# Chapter 10

# *Fundamentalists*

1

Buckland is often dismissed as a belated fundamentalist, but in the context of early nineteenth-century England he was no such thing. In fact fundamentalism, in the sense of a dogmatic insistence on the literal truth of Genesis and on the scriptural time-scale, first acquired a coherent body of propaganda in an effort to counteract the influence of Buckland and his master Cuvier.[1] That the scriptural Flood was the one and only global cataclysm, that all fossils and fossiliferous rocks dated from then and were therefore less than six thousand years old – these things were vigorously reaffirmed in the 1820s, in conscious opposition to Buckland's theses.

The first important leader of the fundamentalist party was Granville Penn.[2] Penn was a serious scholar who had studied geology and was able to use a number of geological facts in his attempt to undermine current geological theory. From his *Comparative Estimate of the Mineral and Mosaic Geologies* of 1822 to his *Conversations on Geology* of 1828 he argued that all geology is to be found in Genesis; that the six days of Creation were six literal days; and that the earth is rather less than six thousand years old. The many 'revolutions' postulated by Cuvier had never taken place – in reality there had been only two such. Both were supernatural events, and all important geological phenomena were the results of one or other of those miracles. Originally, God had depressed

portions of the earth's surface and filled them with sea; exactly
1,656 years later he elevated the depressed portions and
depressed what had hitherto been dry land. The result was the
Flood, which swamped the land. It was during those 1,656 years
that God had created human beings and animals; now all (except
for the select company in the ark) perished. During the Flood the
former sea-bed became dry land, ready to be inhabited by future
generations.[3]

Penn claimed to have attained these insights by combining
Genesis with Newtonian physics, and he was certain that the result
was the truth – the only truth: 'Beyond the limit of this Scheme, is
the region of shadow and phantasm.' Many educated readers
were persuaded. But it was George Bugg who produced the classic
formulation of what soon became known as 'scriptural theology'.
In his two-volume work, itself called *Scriptural Geology; or, Geological
Phenomena consistent only with the literal Interpretation of the Sacred
Scriptures, upon the subjects of the Creation and the Deluge* (1826–7),
he showed himself a more radical fundamentalist than Penn. For
him Genesis was a wholly adequate guide to truth:

> The author commenced this discussion under the full convic-
> tion that the Mosaic narrative was LITERALLY CORRECT.
> . . . He has lived nearly forty years under the full and firm belief
> that the Scriptures are strictly and literally true.[4]

And again:

> I allow . . . that Sacred writers may be silent about science and
> even ignorant of it . . . They were under divine and super-
> natural guidance, and therefore personal *ignorance* in the *writer*
> is no *defect*; and *error* is impossible.[5]

By claiming that the earth was immensely old, and had undergone many 'revolutions' before mankind was created, Cuvier
and Buckland had introduced 'a most unaccountable and dangerous mysticism into the interpretation of the Scriptures'. Indeed
they had – Cuvier deliberately, Buckland unconsciously – oper-

ated as enemies of Christianity. And this was true of geologists in general:

> Geology is the *last* subject to which the adversaries of *Revelation* have resorted, and from which as a science of an ambiguous and not very tangible character, they perhaps hoped to derive some objections to its truth . . . And no doubt when the subject should have become sufficiently general and adequately rooted, they would (could they not have been resisted,) have turned our Geology against our Bible, and made us pay dearly for our unwise and easy credulity.[6]

Everything that geologists sought to explain – including fossils – was adequately accounted for by the Flood. In fact the story of the Flood totally disproved the contentions of the geologists; for, as we know from Genesis, the waters came from underground, and rose at the rate of 700 feet a day. These facts were wholly incompatible with the findings of geology – which must therefore be wrong. The Flood was miraculous; and 'if I am asked, *how* the Deluge operated . . . I can only answer that I do not know: for He who *alone* knows, has not told us.'[7]

It was in the 1830s that the 'scriptural geologists' were at their most active – and their attacks were aimed not only at Cuvier and Buckland but at all those thinkers, from Buffon to Lyell, who had minimized the importance of the Flood. George Fairholme, in his *General View of the Geology of Scripture* (1833), argued that all geology since the mid-eighteenth century had been misled by the theories of the earth set forth by Continental philosophers – especially the 'madness' of Buffon. Already in this book the Flood looms large, and it loomed still larger in the *New and Conclusive Physical Demonstration both of the Fact and Period of the Mosaic Deluge and of its having been the only Event of the Kind that has ever occurred upon the Earth* (1837). Here Fairholme went so far as to claim that geologists who deny the uniqueness of the Flood 'practically deny the authenticity, or truth of the revealed covenant'.[8] The purpose of the Flood was to punish 'the moral guilt of the human race' (even though, unavoidably, the animals also perished); so why should God have sent floods before mankind existed? Geologists who claimed immense antiquity for the earth, a long, long history, punctuated by cataclysms, were in error: 'We find that the combined efforts, even of the ablest men, have proved totally incompetent successfully to contend against the simple yet unbending Words of Eternal Truth.'[9]

Other writers hammered the point home.[10] Nevertheless, by the end of the decade the fundamentalist interpretation of the Flood was beginning to lose its appeal. In 1839 John Pye Smith, Principal of Homerton Divinity College, London, published *On the Relation between the Holy Scripture and Some Parts of Geological Science*, in which he unreservedly accepted the findings of scientific geology. He also offered what was (mistakenly) thought to be a novel interpretation of the Genesis story: the Flood was limited to a small area of the earth's surface – but was nevertheless universal in that it practically exterminated mankind, because the area affected was the only one inhabited by human beings.[11]

Smith's view soon became the orthodox view. It was favoured, for instance, by the Savilian Professor of Geometry at Oxford, Baden Henry Baden-Powell, in the article 'Deluge' which he contributed to Kitto's *Cyclopaedia of Biblical Literature* (1845).[12] It was adopted by the bishops and clergy of the Church of England in the *The Bible Commentary* of 1871. And in the United States Edward Hitchcock, President of Amherst College and also Professor of Geology and Natural Theology, lavished enthusiastic praise on Smith in his highly influential *Religion of Geology and Its Connected Sciences* (1851). On both sides of the Atlantic it was very generally accepted by educated people that 'the Noachian Deluge was a local one, though sufficiently extensive in its area to destroy all the then existing race of men'.[13]

But if the fundamentalist view of the Flood was in abeyance, it was not extinct. In fact the twentieth century has witnessed a great resurgence of fundamentalism, especially in the United States: the literal truth of the Genesis story of the Flood has been maintained in innumerable American writings. The tradition launched by the numerous works of George McCready Price, from *Fundamentals of Geology* (1913) to *The Modern Flood Theory of Geology* (1935), is still flourishing today.

A detailed survey of this body of literature would be as wearisome to read as to write. A glance at what is probably the most popular of all fundamentalist treatments of the Flood will suffice to convey its tenor: *The Genesis Flood: The Biblical Record and its Scientific Implications*, by a professor of Old Testament, John C. Whitcomb Jnr, and a professor of hydraulic engineering, Henry M. Morris. This work was first published in 1961 and has never been out of print since. It is the founding document of what in the United States is known as 'creation science' – in reality a body of fundamentalist doctrine, in which 'flood geology' holds a central place. Its treatment of the fossil record is typical.

As is well known, the geological record of fossils follows one and the same order throughout the world: the oldest rocks contain only single-celled creatures, then come invertebrates, then fishes, then dinosaurs, then large mammals. But how can this be, if God created all creatures within a few days, literally understood? For Whitcomb and Morris the Flood offers a solution – or rather a choice of solutions. In the Flood the denser and more stream-lined creatures would have sunk more rapidly, so of course they would populate the bottom strata. Again, the denizens of the ocean would have been overcome first and so would have been the first to sink, while creatures on the mountain-tops would have survived longer, and would therefore now figure in the upper strata. Also, the more intelligent and mobile animals would have fought hardest against being drowned, and so would have ended up on top of the pile. The fact that none of this fits the actual geological record is ignored.

Whitcomb and Morris also propound solutions to problems arising from the biblical story itself. Sceptics have sometimes asked how animals in remote regions could have found their way to the ark, and how the tiny handful of human beings in the ark could have fed so many animals and cleaned out their stalls. This is how those queries are answered in *The Genesis Flood*:

We suggest that . . . Even as God instructed Noah, by specific revelation, concerning the coming Flood and his means of escape from it, so he instructed certain of the animals, through impartation of a migratory directional instinct which would afterwards be inherited in greater or lesser degree by their descendants, to flee from their native habitats to the place of safety. Then, having entered the Ark, they also received from God the power to become more or less dormant, in various ways, in order to be able to survive for a year in which they were to be confined within the Ark while the great storms and convulsions raged outside.[14]

Such arguments have proved astonishingly influential – yet all fundamentalist literature together has probably made less impact than the television film *In Search of Noah's Ark*. First shown in the United States in 1977, this film claims to be a documentary but is in fact a piece of fundamentalist propaganda. To a survey of attempts to find Noah's ark on Mount Ararat it appends the comments that 'the ark is there' and that the story of the ark is 'impeccably true'.

The argument of *In Search of Noah's Ark* has been effectively demolished by others.[15] But the very fact that people have tried to find the ark – often at great inconvenience to themselves – shows how compelling fundamentalist belief can be.

2

There is a lot of history behind the notion that the ark could be on Mount Ararat.[16]

There is no way of knowing whether the earliest Mesopotamian versions of the Flood story – the Sumerian tale of Ziusdra, the Babylonian tale of Atrahasis – mentioned any particular spot as the landing site of the wonderful boat; the tablets are too incomplete. In the *Epic of Gilgamesh* the boat comes to rest on Mount Nisir in the Zagros range. No mountain now bears the name Nisir, but the Zagros Mountains are known: they lie to the east of the river Tigris. One can be rather more precise. Ashurnasirpal II of Assyria (883–859 BCE) knew of Mount Nisir, and he located it to the south of the Little Zab River, which is a tributary of the Tigris on the eastern bank. It may well be that the mountain is the one now known as Pira Magrun, which is 9,000 feet high.

The Genesis version knows nothing of Mount Nisir or of the Zagros range – the ark's landing-site is in 'the mountains of Ararat'. But it is difficult to know what was meant by that. When the Genesis story was composed Ararat was a kingdom to the north of Mesopotamia, somewhere around Lakes Van and Urmia in modern Turkey; in Assyrian records it is called Urartu. In the last centuries BCE and the early centuries CE translators of Genesis often translated Ararat by 'Armenia' – naturally enough, since by that time Armenia occupied roughly the same area as the ancient kingdom of Urartu/Ararat. However, there was still an Ararat: a small, northerly district of Armenia was so called, and it contained that impressive peak now called Mount Ararat or Great Ararat (Aghri Daghri in Turkish).

Christians were very slow to identify that mountain as the landing-site of the ark: it was only at the end of the middle ages that the idea became widespread. However, by that time it was also widely believed that remnants of the ark were still there. Not that anybody saw them. Great Ararat is nearly 17,000 feet high. Its peak is perpetually covered in snow and ice, with glaciers hundreds of feet thick; and much of the lower terrain is steep and rugged, with plenty of loose rocks, and poisonous snakes amongst the rocks. A hard mountain to climb, even today – and before modern times, practically impossible. There was in fact a tradition amongst the Armenian population that it was not only impossible but forbidden by God. It was said that St Jacob, Bishop of Nisibis, tried to climb the mountain to see the ark but was turned back by an angel; his ambition ran contrary to the Lord's wish. It was a sign of God's compassion that the angel gave Jacob a piece of wood from the ark, by way of consolation.[17]

In the seventeenth century a German scholar, Adam Olearius, wrote of the travels he had undertaken and the observations he had made while serving as ambassador to Muscovy and Persia. The Armenians and Persians, he reported, were convinced that there were still remnants of the ark on Ararat; in Persia he had even been shown a cross made of hard, black wood, which was said to come from the ark, and was cherished accordingly.[18] By the seventeenth century, too, Christian monks were coming from afar to live as hermits on the sacred mountain. As a reward for curing one of those hermits of a hernia, a Dutch traveller, Jan Janzoon Struys, received 'a piece of wood of the true ark of Noah'.[19] Struys also learned that people were making a medicinal powder from the pitch with which Noah coated the ark.

It was only in the nineteenth century that anyone really managed to reach the summit of Mount Ararat. In 1829 Johann Jacob Friedrich Wilhelm Parrot, a professor at the University of Dorpat in Estonia (then part of the Russian empire), tried but failed to find the ark, and had to content himself with erecting a wooden cross on the summit and holding a prayer-meeting there with his companions. Other adventurous spirits followed and likewise erected crosses. In 1845 a geologist called Hermann Abich – also from the University of Dorpat – made a successful ascent and erected a cross. In 1850 a Colonel Khodzko led a force of sixty Russian soldiers up the mountain and erected yet another cross.

In the course of the twentieth century several sightings of the ark, or of remnants of it, have been reported. Two examples will suffice. In 1941–2 three American religious magazines reported that many years earlier, in 1916, a Russian airman named Vladimir Roskovitsky had seen the remains of the ark on a slope when he flew over Mount Ararat. The Tsar was said to have been so impressed that he commissioned an expedition, which climbed the mountain and really found the ark. This was supposed to have happened in 1917 – an unfortunate year, for the expedition's report had naturally been lost in the turmoil of the Russian Revolution. True, the *Chicago Sunday Tribune* later (29 March 1953) announced that, so far from being lost, the report had been deposited, by an aide to the Grand Duke Cyril, in the library of the University of Geneva; but a year's search by a convinced believer, John Warwick Montgomery, failed to find it.[20] So when two of the American religious magazines retracted the whole story they were doing no more than their duty.

Between 1952 and 1969 a French industrialist and amateur explorer, Fernand Navarra, ascended Mount Ararat several times, and claimed to have found traces of the ark. In 1952 he saw a huge black patch in the ice, shaped like a ship's hull (though originally the ark was imagined as a rectangular box). On later occasions he dug down into the ice and found hand-tooled pieces of wood. The results were published in French and in English in 1974.[21] However, when Navarra's piece of wood was subjected to carbon 14 tests, it turned out to date from the seventh century CE at the earliest.[22]

Yet hope persists that the ark will indeed be found.[23] There is nothing strange about that. For, though modern theologians may treat the Genesis story as a religious myth, for multitudes of Christians it is still what it was for so many of the thinkers studied in this book: an absolutely authoritative account of a divinely ordained historical event.

There is nothing strange about that either. Since the days of Hutton and Kirwan 'the deep abyss of time' has become immeasurably deeper, the minuteness of human history far more evident. But for those armed with fundamentalist belief, that bottomless pit is simply not there. Six thousand years since the original Creation, four thousand since that second creation, the Flood – these are reassuring thoughts. And however tragic the story of the Flood itself, it does at least allow a central place to mankind, its past salvation, its assured future – also reassuring thoughts.

# Chapter 11

## *Hidden Meanings Again*

While fundamentalists were insisting on the most literal possible interpretation of the Genesis story, a number of intellectuals were exerting themselves to prove that the story had a hidden meaning.

As to what that meaning was, opinions varied according to the prevailing intellectual climate. At the beginning of the twentieth century solar and solar/lunar interpretations of myth and religion were in vogue;[1] and there were many – including some serious scholars – who persuaded themselves that the true, original meaning of Noah's Flood must lie in the movements of the sun and moon. One such was the celebrated Professor of Assyriology at Leipzig, Heinrich Zimmern. In his contribution to the article 'Deluge' in the authoritative *Encyclopaedia Biblica* (London, 1899) he recognized happily enough that the Genesis story is derived from Babylonian myth – but then he added:

> . . . the great catastrophe is placed by the Babylonians in the middle of the winter season, in the eleventh month . . . To the present writer it seems most probable that the Deluge-story was originally a nature-myth, representing the phenomenon of winter, which in Babylonia especially is a time of rain. The hero rescued in the ship must originally have been a sun-god.[2]

Zimmern's theory had a rival. In a long essay in the highly reputable *Archiv für Religionswissenschaft* a Catholic priest called

Ernst Böklen argued, with great learning, that the ark was the moon, sailing serenely across the heavenly ocean. The loading of the ark symbolized the waxing of the moon, the eight persons who were saved referred to the first quarter of the moon, the three stories in which the vessel was built represented the phases of the moon, so did the animals in the ark, and so, yet again, did the wandering raven and the dove. As for the pitch with which the ark was caulked, that stood for a lunar eclipse. The god who summoned up the Flood was of course the sun-god – but Noah, on the other hand, was the moon-god; and his sons too stood for the moon's phases. As for the bow which the sun-god set in the sky, as a token of his goodwill – that was not, as commonly supposed, the rainbow but the crescent moon.[3]

When Zimmern and Böklen wrote, quite a different kind of nature-religion was about to move into the centre of interest. First published in 1890, reissued with enlargements in twelve volumes between 1907 and 1915, James Frazer's *Golden Bough* launched a veritable cult of nature-cults. At least in the English-speaking world it became fashionable to see in the most diverse gods and heroes so many disguises for the spirit of vegetation. It was to be expected that this kind of interpretation would be applied also to the story of the Flood – and so it was. In 1939 there appeared in *Religions*, the journal of the London-based Society for the Study of Religions, a paper by Eleanor Follansbee in which it is argued, with more erudition than judgment, that the story of the Flood originated not in Babylonia but in Syria. In Syria, however, floods bring not devastation but fertility – so the Syrian prototype of Noah must surely have been 'the king-god who is bound up with the principle of growth, Tammuz'. Drawing on the myth-ritual theory, which at that time was still taken seriously, the author carried the argument further. Noah's forty days in the ark, she suggested, might correspond to Tammuz' imprisonment in the netherworld; for, like Tammuz, Noah returns 'to bring back life to earth'.[4]

Meanwhile the story of the Flood was being subjected to psychoanalytical interpretation. Already in 1912 one of Freud's earliest followers, Otto Rank, tackled the matter in the yearbook for psychoanalytical research. After interpreting a number of dreams as disguised fantasies of urination, Rank went on to apply the same approach to flood myths. Amongst these he distinguished between simple myths based on fantasies of pissing and those which combined fantasies of pissing with fantasies of being born and of sex. The former, he reckoned, were typical of 'primitive' peoples. The supreme example of the latter, on the other hand, was the Genesis story – for while the Flood itself clearly had a urinary origin, what could the ark be if not the maternal womb, and what could the exit from the ark be if not birth, to be followed in due course by procreation?[5]

Depth-psychological interpretation of the Flood continued.[6] In 1944 the American Jungian analyst Eleanor Bertine saw in flood myths in general, and the Genesis story in particular, expressions of a psychic process. The flood stands for the unconscious, which is both dangerous and a potential source of healing:

> . . . the unconscious is the greatest peril to consciousness, while also being a source of regeneration. The flood comes at the moment of crisis. To the majority it spells destruction, to the hero rebirth. Which it shall be depends upon whether the spark of divine wisdom within him enables a man to orient himself positively to the experience of the waters, accepting them as a suprapersonal reality capable of bringing renewal. Such an orientation or adaptation is symbolized by the ark or chest or boat. In this he may ride out the deluge and emerge to a new heaven and a new earth. Thus he becomes the twice-born . . .[7]

Writing some forty years later, the distinguished American folk-lorist Alan Dundes viewed the story from a very different point of view. For him flood myths constitute 'a cosmogonic projection of the standard means by which every child-bearing female creates. It is the bursting of the sac releasing the amniotic fluids which announce the birth of each newborn baby.' Not that the flood simply represents the amniotic fluid – it expresses the uncon-scious wish of man to be able to produce, from his penis, a comparably significant flow: 'flood myths are an example of males seeking to imitate female creativity.' And from this premise femi-nist conclusions are drawn: 'The flood myth in Genesis belongs to a patriarchal period of human history and as such constitutes a sacred charter for man's privileged position in the world.' And if male scholars, including theologians, spend so much time and energy on such documents, that is because, 'increasingly threat-ened by what they perceive as angry females dissatisfied with ancient myths which give priority to males [they] cling desperately to these traditional expressions of mythopoeic magic.'[8]

Such are some of the multifarious interpretations of Noah's Flood that have been offered in the course of the twentieth cen-tury. Not one of them shows any awareness of the thought which obsessed the men who composed the Genesis story and which continued to obsess generation after generation of Christians: the thought of a wrathful God intent on punishing a sinful mankind, cleansing a corrupted world, and making a fresh start. Still, these latterday interpretations are not without interest. Appearing in such rapid succession, sometimes even flourishing side by side, yet mostly inconsistent with one another, they do prove this much: that the story of Noah's Flood can still call forth quite remarkable intellectual exertions and inspire quite remarkable ingenuity – as it has been doing for some two thousand years.

# Appendix

# Contemporary Criticism of Burnet's and Whiston's Interpretations of the Flood

Would-be scientific theories about the Flood have commonly evoked queries, objections, rival theories – and that happened already with the pioneering efforts of Burnet and Whiston: if both were hailed as major discoveries, both were also widely denounced. The Latin version of Burnet's book met with a rejoinder, from Germany, as early as 1683. The English version was countered by Herbert Croft, Bishop of Hereford, in 1685: he branded the book a 'Philosophick Romance', full of 'extravagant Fancies', 'vain Fopperies', and 'fabulous Inventions', and designed to subvert the scriptures and the Church.[1] The Flood was a miracle, and called for no explanation: 'let it be unintelligible; Is it a good consequence therefore to say it is Incredible?'[2]

A more effective reply came in the same year (1690) as the publication of the English translation of the enlarged version, in the shape of *Geologia: or, a Discourse Concerning the Earth before the Deluge*, by Erasmus Warren, rector of Warlington in Suffolk. (According to the *Oxford English Dictionary* the use of the word 'geology' to denote a distinct branch of physical science began with that title.) The biblical account of creation, Warren insisted, was to be understood literally: the long, slow process suggested by Burnet never took place. Moreover his theory about the altered surface of the earth, 'which geography hitherto never dreamed of', was demonstrably false: if the earth had ever been without sea, Adam would not have had dominion over the fish in the sea. As for the Flood, Warren has his own theory. The water came from great caverns in the high rocks, where it had been stored from the beginning of the world. Nor was the amount of water required overwhelmingly large: the measurement of fifteen cubits referred to the height of the Flood above the 'common surface' of the earth, not above lofty mountains like the Swiss Alps. Even a moderate amount of water would have sufficed to exterminate all living creatures, as they would have been unable to escape by scaling the peaks – the darkness and the rains rushing down the slopes would have seen to that. Above all, Warren insists that, so far from being a ruin, the present earth is beautiful: its very unevenness makes it far more beautiful than the supposedly smooth earth before the Flood could possibly have been.

The publication of Whiston's book prompted John Keill, Savilian Professor of Astronomy at Oxford, to produce a vigorous critique, *An Examination of Dr Burnet's Theory of the Earth. Together with some remarks on Mr Whiston's New Theory of the Earth* (1698). Keill condemns both writers as 'world-makers', 'flood-makers' – makers of imaginary worlds and loosers of imaginary floods. These and other 'moderns', he asserts, follow in the footsteps of Descartes, 'the first world-maker this Century produced'; and like him they claim to 'have discovered Nature in all her works, and can tell you the true cause of every effect, from the sole principles of matter and motion. If you will believe them, they can inform you exactly, how God made the world.'[3]

The error of such thinkers is twofold. In their eagerness to harmonize Genesis and natural philosophy they in effect deny the need for 'any extraordinary concurrence of the Divine Power'.[4] And even their natural philosophy (or science, as we would call it) is defective, since it is based not on patient observation, interpreted in the light of geometry, but on mere 'fantasy'. All this is true of their treatment of the Flood:

Thus we see how these flood-makers have given the Atheists an argument to uphold their cause; which I think can only be truely answer'd by proving an universal deluge from Mechanical causes altogether impossible.... This I intend to do by shewing that their Theories are neither consonant to the established laws of motion, nor to acknowledged principles of natural Philosophy ... founded upon observations and calculations.[5]

And so he does. Against Burnet's *Theory of the Earth* he deploys formidable forces – not only his own mathematical knowledge, which was considerable, but also such leading scientific authorities as Kepler, Boyle, and especially Newton. What emerges is that nothing is the result of chance, everything reveals the divine purpose. If the earth's axis is not upright, that is because God placed it, at the creation, in the best possible position. Likewise the earth's surface, including its mountains, is designed by God to serve mankind. The ante-diluvian earth of Burnet's imagining – smooth, without seas or mountains, bathed in perpetual sunlight – would be absolutely uninhabitable. Despite Burnet's merits as a writer, his 'lofty and plausible stile', his book is nothing but a 'Philosophical Romance'.[6]

Keill offers a very different vision. The true explanation of the Flood, he insists, is to be found not in 'mechanical causes' but in the sovereign will and power of God:

> Is any thing of this nature too hard for the Almighty to perform? ... Why ought we to deny this universal destruction of the earth to be miraculous? ... It is therefore both the easiest and safest way, to refer the wonderful destruction of the old world to the Omnipresent hand of God, who can do whatsoever he pleases.[7]

Keill treats Whiston with more respect than Burnet – as well he might, for he was himself a Newtonian and indeed a member of Newton's inner circle. He even grants that Whiston has proved that a comet passed close by the earth on the very day the Flood began, 812 years after the Creation. However, he does not accept that the comet could possibly have produced the Flood. Nor can he accept that the earth itself was originally a comet – for comets are luminous, whereas Scripture states that after the earth was created, darkness was still on the face of the deep.[8] Keill concludes by inviting Whiston, as a man of candour and sincerity, to further discussion of these matters.

Whiston did in fact reply, in two volumes (1698 and 1700), and so did Burnet, in 1699, and Keill replied to both, also in 1699. By 1700 the controversy provoked by Burnet and Whiston had involved some twenty authors in addition to the principals.[9] And the debate was continued on the Continent: in the second half of the eighteenth century thinkers of the stature of Buffon and Voltaire still thought it worth their while to take part.[10]

# Notes

The Notes include both bibliographical references and matters of academic rather than of general interest. Works are in general listed in the chronological order of their first publication. At the first mention of a work the full title, place of publication (or alternatively, name of university press) and date of first publication are given. Later mentions, unless far removed, are abbreviated.

## Foreword

1. J. Riem, *Die Sintflut in Sage und Wissenschaft*, Hamburg, 1925, Teil 2, 'Die Berichte', contains over three hundred stories. The first volume of James Frazer, *Folklore in the Old Testament*, London, 1918, includes a generous (though not exhaustive) survey of flood stories; for a valuable collection of extracts from this see Theodor H. Gaster, *Myth, Legend, and Custom in the Old Testament*, New York and London, 1969, 82–131. Chapter 7 of Dorothy B. Vitaliano, *Legends of the Earth. Their Geologic Origin*, Indiana University Press, 1973, contains an instructive transcultural survey. Many of the essays in Alan Dundes (ed.), *The*

*Flood Myth*, University of California Press, 1988 – an invaluable work – are also relevant.

2. Francis L. Utley, 'Noah, his wife and the Devil', in Raphael Patai et al. (eds), *Studies in Biblical and Jewish Folklore*, University of Indiana Press, 1960, 59–91. The article has a wider range than its title would suggest. The passage quoted is at p. 86.

## Chapter 1: Mesopotamian Origins

1. Cf. Harold Peake, *The Flood. New Light on an Old Story*, London, 1930; André Parrot, *The Flood and Noah's Ark*, London, 1955 (from the French, 1953); Max E.L. Mallowan, 'Noah's Flood

reconsidered', in *Iraq* 26 (1964), 62–82; Robert L. Raikes, 'The physical evidence for Noah's Flood', in *Iraq* 28 (1966), 52–63. For a survey of alternative hypotheses: Lloyd R. Bailey, *Noah. The Person and the Story in History and Tradition*, University of South Carolina Press, 1989, 28–51.

2. Shurrupak is referred to in *Gilgamesh* XI, and the Ziusdra who figures in the short poem in Sumerian summarized here was in fact king of Shurrupak.

3. Trans. Miguel Civil, in Lambert and Millard (see Note 4), at pp. 140–5. The quotation is taken from pp. 143, 145.

4. The British Museum copy consists of some 1,245 lines in cuneiform script. Although it has been available since the mid-nineteenth century, it has been correctly read only since 1956. The standard translation is Wilfred G. Lambert and Alan R. Millard, *Atra-hasis. The Babylonian Story of the Flood*, Oxford University Press, 1969. The valuable introduction includes an account of the discovery and reconstruction of the text; on the latter see also Jørgen Laessoe, 'The Atrahasis Epic: A Babylonian History of Mankind', in *Bibliotheca Orientalis* 13 (1956), 90–102. A complete copy of the myth is reported to have been discovered by Iraqi archaeologists working at the site of Sippar, but it had not been published by 1994.

The account of *Atrahasis* in the present chapter owes much to publications which appeared in the wake of the Lambert/ Millard translation, notably the article by Wolfram von Soden, 'Als die Götter (auch noch)

Mensch waren. Einige Grundgedanken des altbabylonischen Atramhasis-Mythus', in *Orientalia* 38 (1969), 415–532; and the review article by William L. Moran in *Biblica* 52 (1971), 51–61. Giovanni Pettinato, 'Die Bestrafung des Menschengeschlechts . . .', in *Orientalia* 37 (1968), 165–200, argued that the noisiness of mankind was tantamount to a sinful revolt against the divinely established order; but this view has not found general acceptance.

A good and recent translation of *Gilgamesh* is that by Maureen G. Kovacs, Stanford University Press, 1985. Jeffrey H. Tigay, *The Evolution of the Gilgamesh Epic*, University of Pennsylvania Press, 1982, has a chapter on the Flood story.

5. Harry A. Hoffner, 'Enki's command to Atrahasis', in *Alter Orient und Altes Testament* 25 (1976) (Kramer Anniversary Volume) argues that the *Gilgamesh* version is based on a misunderstanding of the original. The description of the Flood is taken from Tablet XI of *Gilgamesh*, lines 96 seq. in Kovacs.

6. Cf. Anne D. Kilmer, 'The Mesopotamian concept of overpopulation and its solution as reflected in mythology', in *Orientalia* 41 (1972), 160–77; and Moran, op. cit. Erle V. Lichty, 'Demons and population control', in *Expedition* 13 No. 2, University of Pennsylvania: University Museum, 1971, 22–6, is also relevant.

The literature of ancient India provides a curious parallel to this part of *Atrahasis*. The story as told in the *Mahabharata* (twice, at VII 52–54 and XII 256 seq.) goes as follows. Mankind, created by

Brahma, multiplied to the point that it became an intolerable burden to Earth, who complained to Brahma. Perplexed, then furious, Brahma decided to annihilate mankind. But the god Shiva intervened and begged Brahma to think again. As a result of Brahma's meditation a beautiful, black-eyed woman came forth from his body; and Brahma appointed her Goddess of Death, with the task of killing young and old, rich and poor, the stupid and the clever alike. But the goddess, appalled at the thought of the hatred she would incur from mortals, wept bitterly. Moved by her tears, Brahma created various Messengers of Death: hatred, greed, violence, jealousy, envy, wasting diseases were to assist in the task. So the Goddess of Death is never blamed by human beings, but on the contrary welcomed, as they recognize that she spares them all sorts of misery. Cf. Haim Schwarzbaum, 'The overcrowded earth', in *Numen* 4 (1957) 59–74 at 62–3.

7.  Cf. Benno Landsberger, in a discussion on scribal concepts of education in Carl H. Kraeling and Robert M. Adams (eds), *City Invincible*, University of Chicago, Oriental Institute, 1960, 94 seq.

8.  Cf. Dorothy B. Vitaliano, *Legends of the Earth. Their Geologic Origins*, Indiana University Press, 1973, 158.

9.  Ovid, *Metamorphoses* I, lines 261–415.

10.  For an exhaustive survey of Graeco-Roman versions: Gian Andrea Caduff, *Antike Sintflutsagen*, Göttingen, 1986. On their debt to Near Eastern models: ibid., 129 seq.

## Chapter 2: The Genesis Story

1.  For an exhaustive commentary on Genesis 6–9, with bibliography, see Klaus Westermann, *Genesis 1–11*, London, 1984 (from the German, 1974). The Flood is at 384–480. Quotations from Genesis in the present chapter are taken from the translation by Ephraim A. Speiser in vol. 1 of *The Anchor Bible*, Garden City, N.Y., 1964.

2.  Genesis 6: 17.

3.  7: 11.

4.  7: 21–23.

5.  8: 22.

6.  9: 16.

7.  9: 1.

8.  8: 17.

9.  For various estimates of the relationship between the Mesopotamian and the biblical stories: Alexander Heidel, *The Gilgamesh Epic and Old Testament Parallels*, University of Chicago Press, 1949; Wilfred G. Lambert, 'A new look at the Babylonian background of Genesis', in *Journal of Theological Studies* 16 (1965), 286–300; Alan R. Millard, 'A new Babylonian 'Genesis' story', in *Tyndale Bulletin* 18 (1966), 3–18; Eugene Fisher, '*Gilgamesh* and Genesis: the Flood story in context', in *Catholic Biblical Quarterly* 32 (1970), 392–403; Tikva Frymer-Kensky, 'The Atrahasis Epic and its significance for our understanding of Genesis', in *The Biblical Archaeologist* 40 (1977), 147–54; and for a concise summary, Bailey (see Note 1 to Chapter 1), 11–20.

No account is taken here of the version of the Mesopotamian story by the Babylonian priest

Berossus, as it is too late (third century BCE) to have influenced Genesis.

10. Genesis 6: 11–13.

11. On the relationship between the J and P contributions see, in addition to Westermann, op. cit., and Bailey, op. cit.; W.J. Dalton, 'The background and meaning of the Biblical Flood Narrative', in *Australian Catholic Record* 34 (1957) 292–304 ad fin. and esp. 35 (1958), 23–39; Sean E. McEvenue, *The Narrative Style of the Priestly Writer*, Rome, 1971, chapters 2 and 3; David L. Petersen, 'The Yahwist and the Flood', in *Vetus Testamentum* 26 (1976), 438–46; Gordon J. Wenham, 'The coherence of the Flood narrative', in *Vetus Testamentum* 28 (1978), 336–48; George W. Coats, *Genesis, with an Introduction to Narrative Literature*, vol. 1, Grand Rapids, 1983, 73–84.

12. Jeremiah 4: 23–5 (NEB).

13. On the connection between P and the experience of exile: Walter Brueggemann, 'The kerygma of the Priestly writers', in *Zeitschrift für die alttestamentliche Wissenschaft* 84 (1972), 328–413; J. Blenkinsopp, 'The structure of P', in *Catholic Biblical Quarterly* 38 (1976) 275–92, esp. 283 seq.

14. For a brief account of the transformation see N. Cohn, *Cosmos, Chaos and the World to Come*, Yale University Press, 1993, Chapter 8, esp. 148 seq.; for fuller accounts see the works listed in Note 1 to that chapter.

15. On George Smith: E.A. Wallis Budge, *The Rise and Progress of Assyriology*, London, 1925, 106–19; R. Campbell Thompson, *A Century of Exploration at Nineveh*, London, 1929, 48–54. For Smith's own account of his discovery: *The Chaldaean Account of Genesis* (published posthumously, ed. Archibald H. Sayce), London, 1876; and for an early (and favourable) reaction: Sayce, 'The Chaldaean account of the Deluge and its relation to the Old Testament', in *Theological Review* 10 (1872), 364–77.

## Chapter 3: Hidden Meanings

In the notes to this chapter the following abbreviations are used: PG for *Patrologia Graeca*; PL for *Patrologia Latina*; CSEL for *Corpus Scriptorum Ecclesiasticorum Latinorum*.

1. Cf. Geoffrey W.H. Lampe and Kenneth J. Woollcombe, *Essays on Typology*, London, 1957. The quotation is from Lampe, ibid., p. 15, with Augustine at p. 13. Woollcombe's essay. 'The biblical origin and patristic development of typology', is also relevant.

   For an old but comprehensive treatment of Jewish and Christian typology down the ages see Frederic W. Farrar, *History of Interpretation*, London, 1886.

2. On early Christian exegesis of Genesis 6–9: Jean Daniélou, *Sacramentum Futuri. Études sur les origines de la typologie biblique*, Paris, 1950, 54–94; Jack P. Lewis, *A Study of the Interpretation of Noah and the Flood in Jewish and Christian Literature*, Leiden, 1968, 101–20, 156–80.

3. Matthew 24: 37–9; cf. Luke 17: 26–7. Quotations from the New Testament are taken from the RSV.

4. II Peter 3: 5–7.

5. Hebrews 11: 1, 7.

6. II Peter 2: 5; I Clement 7. 6.

7. Theophilus of Antioch, *Ad Autolycum* III. 19 (PG 6, 1146–48).

8. Cf. Augustine, *De catechizandis rudibus* XIX. 32 (PL 40, 334); John Chrysostom, *In Epistolam I Thessalonicenses Commentarius cap. 4 Homilia VIII.* 2 (PG 62, 442).

9. II Peter 3: 9–10.

10. Justin, *Apologia II.* 5 (PG 6, 452).

11. Origen, *Homilia in Ezechielem IV.* 8 (PG 13, 703); *idem, Contra Celsum,* IV. 41 (PG 11, 1096).

12. *Constitutiones Apostolorum,* VIII. 12. 22, in Franz Xaver Funk, *Didiscalia et Constitutiones Apostolorum,* Paderborn, 1895 (at p. 503).

13. Matthew 11: 28–29.

14. Cyril of Jerusalem, *Catechesis XVII, De Spiritu Sancto,* 10 (PG 33. 981 A); Ephraem Syrus, *Hymns on the Nativity 1 (A Select Library of Nicene and Post-Nicene Fathers of the Christian Church,* series II. 13. 225); Cyril of Alexandria, *Glaphyrorum in Genesim lib. II.* 5 (PG 69, 65 B–C); Augustine, *In Ioannis Evangelium Tractatus IX.* 11 (PL 35. 1464).

15. Justin, *Dialogus cum Tryphone* 138 (PG 6, 793).

16. Irenaeus, *Adversus Haereses* V. 29 (PG 7, 1202).

17. Origen, *Homilia in Genesim II.* 3, 4 (PG 12, 167–9).

18. Augustine, *De Civitate Dei* XV. 24. This long quotation is taken, with a few small changes, from the admirable translation by Demetrius B. Zema and Gerald G. Walsh, in the series *The Fathers of the Church: Augustine, The City of God,* vol. 2, Washington D.C. 1952, 477–9.

19. Cf. Irenaeus, *Adversus Haereses* IV. 36. 4 (PG 7, 1093); Cyprian, *Epistola LXXIV.* 11 (CSEL 3. 2. 808); Jerome, *Epistola XV.* 2 (ibid. 54. 63–4); Augustine, *De catechizandis rudibus* XXVII. 53 (PL 40, 346), cf. *De Civitate* XV. 26.

20. John Chrysostom, *De Lazaro Concio VI* (PG 47, 1037–8).

21. Cyprian *Epistola LXIX.* 2 (CSEL 3.2. 751).

22. Ambrose, repeatedly, e.g. *De Mysteriis* III, 10–11 (PL 26, 392 B).

23. Augustine, *De catechizandis* XIX. 31–32 (PL 40. 333–4).

24. Jerome, *Epistola LXIX.* 6 (CSEL 54, 690).

25. Augustine, *Contra Faustum* 12.20 (CSEL 25. 348); *idem, In Ioannis Evangelium Tractatus VI.* 3 (PL 35.1426).

26. Cf. Erwin R. Goodenough, *Jewish Symbols in the Greco-Roman Period* vol. 2, New York, 1953, 119–20; Joseph Wilpert, *La fede della Chiesa nascente secondo i monumenti dell'arte funeraria antica,* Vatican City, 1938, 129, 218. The standard typological interpretations of the Flood as baptism, the ark as the Church, and the dove as the Holy Spirit are combined in Didymus of Alexandria, *De Trinitate* II (PG 39, 697 A–B).

27. *Book of Adam and Eve* III, 10 (probably fourth century CE).

## Chapter 4: Filling Gaps

1. Cf. Lewis, op. cit., chapter 6, 'The Rabbinic Noah'; Louis Ginzberg, *The Legends of the Jews,* vol. 1, Philadelphia, 1909, 145–69 (with notes in vol. 5 (1925), 167–206).

Lewis can also be profitably consulted for the treatment of Noah and the Flood in the Jewish Apocrypha and by Philo of Alexandria and Josephus – matters which lie outside the scope of the present work.

2. *Genesis Rabbah* 34. 11. This and the following references are to the translation of *Genesis Rabbah* in *Midrash Rabbah* vol. 1, ed. H. Freedman and I. Epstein, London, 1939.

3. 38.6. The quotation is taken from Job 21: 15.

4. 26.4–5; 30.2; 23.2.

5. 28.8.

6. 31.5.

7. 27.2–3.

8. 30.9.

9. 26.6; 29.1.

10. 30.5.

11. For all this: 31: 11.

12. 31: 14.

13. 31.13.

14. 31.13.

15. Cf. Lewis, op. cit., 141.

16. Ibid., 142.

17. Ibid., 144.

18. Ibid., 145.

19. *Genesis Rabbah* 33.5.

20. 33.6.

21. 30.6.

22. Cf. Don Cameron Allen, *The Legend of Noah. Renaissance Rationalism in Art, Science and Letters*, University of Illinois Press, 1949, 71–81.

23. Origen, *Homilia in Genesim II*. 2 (PG 12, 161–2).

24. Procopius of Gaza, *Commentarii in Genesin* (PG 87, 274–5).

25. Bede, *Hexameron* (PL 91, 89–92).

26. Trans. Allen, op. cit., 76.

27. Johanes Buteo, *De arca Noë, cuius formae, capacitatisque fuerit libellus*, in *Opera geometrica*, Lyons, 1554, 7–28.

28. Burton, *The Anatomy of Melancholy* (ed. Shiletto, London, 1891–3), II, 51.

29. Browne, *Works*, ed. Keynes, London. 1928, vol. 1, 31.

30. Cf. Allen (see Note 22 above) 85–9.

31. On La Peyrère: Richard H. Popkin, *Isaac La Peyrère (1596–1676). His Life, Work and Influence*, Leiden. 1987.

32. Isaac Vossius, *Dissertatio de vera aetate mundi*, The Hague, 1659, 53; Georg C. Kirchmaier, *De diluvii universalitate dissertatio prolusoria*, Geneva, 1667, 3–60.

33. Genesis 1: 7.

34. Walter Raleigh, *The History of the World*, London, 1614, 90–1.

35. Athanasius Kircher, *Arca Noë*, Amsterdam, 1675, 201; cf. *Mundus Subterraneus*, vol. 1, Amsterdam, 1664, 70.

36. *Arca Noë*, 129.

## *Chapter 5: A Ruined Earth*

1. Cf. Richard S. Westfall, *Science and Religion in Seventeenth-Century England*, Yale University Press, 1958, esp. Chapter 1.

2. Cf. Margaret C. Jacob, *The Newtonians and the English Revolution, 1689–1720*, Hassocks, 1976, esp. 34 seq.

3. In addition to Allen (see Note 22 to Chapter 4), works which give attention to Burnet and Whiston include, eg, Katharine B. Collier, *Cosmogonies of Our Fathers. Some Theories of the Seventeenth and Eighteenth Centuries*, Columbia University, 1934; Basil Willey, *The Eighteenth-Century Background. Studies on the Idea of Nature in the Thought of the Period*, London,

1940; Michael Macklem, *The Anatomy of the World. Relations between Natural and Moral Law from Donne to Pope*, University of Minnesota Press, 1958; John C. Greene, *The Death of Adam. Evolution and its Impact on Western Thought*, Iowa University Press, 1959; Marjorie H. Nicolson, *Mountain Gloom and Mountain Glory. The Development of the Aesthetics of the Infinite*, Cornell University Press, 1959; Stephen Toulmin and June Goodfield, *The Discovery of Time*, London, 1965; Gordon L. Davies, *The Earth in Decay. A History of British Geomorphology, 1578–1878*, London, 1968; Paolo Rossi, *The Dark Abyss of Time. The History of the Earth and the History of Nations from Hooke to Vico*, University of Chicago Press, 1984 (from the Italian 1979); Stephen J. Gould, *Time's Arrow, Time's Cycle. Myth and Metaphor in the Discovery of Geological Time*, Harvard University Press, 1987; Richard Huggett, *Cataclysms and Earth History. The Development of Diluvialism*, Oxford, Clarendon Press, 1989. Rossi's pioneering study throws much light on ideas about the Flood during the seventeenth and eighteenth centuries as a whole. Another Italian work provides an excellent introduction to Burnet's thought in particular: Mirella Pasini, *Thomas Burnet. Una storia del mondo tra ragione, mito e rivelazione*, Florence, 1981. Also relevant is: Jacques Roger, 'La Théorie de la Terre au XVIIe siècle', in *Revue d'histoire des sciences* 26 (1973), 23–48. For Burnet's millenarianism see Note 20 below.

4.   See p. 24 above.

5.   *The Sacred Theory of the Earth*, 110. All page references are to *The Sacred Theory of the Earth*, 1965, London and Fontwell, which is a reprint of the 1690 *Theory of the Earth*.

6.   *The Sacred Theory of the Earth*, 23.

7.   Ibid., 36.

8.   Ibid., 128–9.

9.   Ibid., 39.

10.   Ibid., 53.

11.   For Burnet's cosmology: ibid., 54 seq. (with some notable illustrations).

12.   Psalms 12: 2; 136: 6.

13.   *The Sacred Theory of the Earth*, 164.

14.   On 'the dissolution of the First Earth': ibid., 65–71.

15.   Ibid., 84.

16.   Ibid., 82, 89.

17.   Ibid., 112.

18.   Ibid., 102.

19.   Ibid., 277, 288.

20.   For two very different interpretations of Burnet's millenarianism: Ernest L. Tuveson, *Millennium and Utopia. A Study of the Background of the Idea of Progress*, University of California Press, 1949; M. C. Jacob and W. A. Lockwood, 'Political Millenarianism and Burnet's *Sacred Theory*', in *Science Studies* 2 (1972), 265–279.

21.   *The Sacred Theory of the Earth*, 93.

22.   Cf. Nicolson, op. cit., chapter 2; Pasini, op. cit., chapter 1.

23.   Goodman, *The Fall of Man*, 280–6.

24.   Michael Drayton, *Poly-Olbion*, Book IX, lines 105–22; Edmund Waller, *Poetical Works*, ed. George Gilfillan, Edinburgh, 1857, 195.

25.   References for the quotations from Warton, Wordsworth and Coleridge are given in Nicolson, op. cit., 194–5.

26.   For the full text of the letter: Herbert W. Turnbull, *The Cor-*

respondence of Isaac Newton, II:
1676–87, Royal Society, 1960,
329–34. Newton's letter is in
reply to a letter from Burnet,
ibid., 321–7.

27. In the *Protogaea* which, though
published only in 1749, was
written in 1690.

28. Op. cit., Part II, 167–8.

29. *Philosophical Transactions of the
Royal Society* 49 (2) (1756), 672–
82.

30. Griffith Hughes, *The Natural History of Barbados*, London, 1750,
3–4.

## Chapter 6: Providential Comets

1. On Whiston: Maureen Farrell,
*William Whiston*, New York, 1981;
James E. Force, *William Whiston,
Honest Newtonian*, Cambridge
University Press, 1985.

2. *Memoirs of the Life and Writings of
Mr. William Whiston . . . Written by
himself*, London, 1749, I, 34.

3. Ibid., I, 38.

4. Letter from John Locke to
William Molyneaux, 22 February
1696/7, quoted in Whiston,
*Memoirs*, 44; *The Works of John
Locke, Esq.*, III, London, 1727, 55.

5. On the influence of the *New
Theory*: Force, op. cit., 28–9, 167–
9, where full references are
given.

6. Whiston, *A Vindication of the New
Theory of the Earth from the Excep-
tions of Mr. John Keill, and others*, 2.

7. Whiston, *A New Theory of the Earth*,
282.

8. Ibid., 296, 293, 297.

9. Ibid., 300–1.

10. Ibid., 357.

11. Ibid., 359.

12. Ibid., 330.

13. Ibid., 339.

14. Ibid., 296.

15. Ibid., 375–8.

16. Ibid., 374.

17. Ibid., 378.

## Chapter 7: Problematic Fossils

1. For good recent accounts of the
debate outlined in this chapter:
Martin J. S. Rudwick, *The Meaning of Fossils. Episodes in the History
of Palaeontology*, London and New
York, 1972, chapters 1 and 2;
Rossi (see Note 3 to Chapter 5),
part 1.

2. Anton-Lazzaro Moro, *De' crostacei
e degli altri corpi marini che si
trovano su' monti, libri due*, Venice,
1740, 9–14.

3. Cf. Tertullian, *Liber de pallio* (PL
2, 1033–4); Pseudo-Eustatius,
*Commentarius in Hexameron* (PG
18, 752); Procopius of Gaza,
*Commentarii in Genesin* (PG 87,
286).

4. For an authoritative account:
'Nicolaus Steno's life and work',
in *Acta Historica Scientiarum
Naturalium Medicinalium* (Copen-
hagen), 15 (1958), 9–86. Jacob
E. Poulsen and Egill Snorrason
(eds), *Nicolaus Steno 1638–1686.
A Re-Consideration by Danish Scientists*, Gentofte, Denmark, 1986,
contains valuable essays.

5. Trans. F. J. Billeskov Jansen, in
Paulsen and Snorrason, op. cit.,
23.

6. *De Solido Intra Solidum Naturaliter
Contento Dissertationis Prodromus*
(first edn), Florence, 1669. English trans. by John G. Winter,
New York, 1916, repr. New York
and London, 1968.

7. Cf. Winter's trans., 228.

8. Ibid., 258–9.
9. Ibid., 266–7.
10. *Nature* 24 (1881), 452.
11. For a good modern account of Woodward's life and work: Joseph M. Levine, *Dr. Woodward's Shield. History, Science and Satire in Augustan England*, University of California Press, 1977, chapters 1–7.
12. *An Attempt toward a Natural History of Fossils*, London, 1729, 1.
13. *An Essay toward a Natural History of the Earth*, 82.
14. Ibid., Preface.
15. Ibid., 117, 163.
16. Ibid., Preface, and 76 seq.
17. Ibid., 80–81.
18. See pp. 47–8 above.
19. Ibid., 166.
20. Ibid., 83–4.
21. Ibid., 91.
22. Ibid., 92.
23. Ibid., 93.
24. Ibid., 84.
25. Ibid., 86.
26. Ibid., 88.
27. Ibid., 88.
28. Ibid., 94.
29. On Scheuchzer: Melvin E. Jahn, 'Notes on Dr Scheuchzer and on Homo diluvii testis', in Cecil J. Schneer (ed.), *Toward a History of Geology*, M.I.T. Press, 1969, 193–213. Rudolf Wolf, *Biographien zur Kulturgeschichte der Schweiz*, Zurich, 1858, vol. 1, contains a biography, which however makes no mention of Scheuchzer's diluvial approach to palaeontology or the blunders it gave rise to.
30. Trans. from *Physica Sacra*, in Melvin E. Jahn and Daniel J. Woolf, *The Lying Stones of Dr. Johann Bartholomew Adam Beringer*, University of California Press, 1963, 173.
31. *Sammlung von Natur- und Medicin-Geschichten* 32, April 1726, 407.
32. Georges Cuvier, *Recherches sur les Ossemens Fossiles*, 3rd edn, Paris, 1825, V, 431–40.

## Chapter 8: Shifting Time-Scales

1. Theophilus of Antioch, *Ad Autolycum*, III. 28 (PG 6. 1163); cf. Augustine, *De Civitate Dei*, XII. 12.

    It was Alexandre Koyré who coined the phrase 'from the closed world to the infinite universe', in the title of his famous book (Baltimore, 1957).
2. Cf. John D. North, 'Chronology and the Age of the World', in Wolfgang Yourgrau and Allen D. Breck, *Chronology, History and Theology*, New York, 1977, 307–33.
3. This description of Moses is taken from Thomas Robinson, *A Vindication of the Philosophical and Theological Exposition of the Mosaick System of Creation*, London, 1709, 54.
4. James Ussher, *The Annals of the Old Testament. From the Beginning of the World*, London, 1658, 1, 3.
5. *Philosophical Transactions of the Royal Society* 36 (1730), 397–424.
6. On Catcott: Katherine B. Collier, *Cosmogonies of Our Fathers*, 234–41; Gordon L. Davies, *The Earth in Decay*, 108–10. (For both see Note 3 to Chapter 5.)
7. Catcott, *A Treatise on the Deluge*, London, 1761, 163.
8. *Treatise on the Deluge*, 2nd edn., London, 1768, 411.
9. In his cosmology, and in his ideas about how the Flood came about,

Catcott was much influenced by John Hutchinson (1674–1739). Hutchinson had started as an assistant to Woodward but later developed a cosmology which, while ostensibly biblical, was really esoteric; cf. Michael Neve and Roy Porter, 'Alexander Catcott. Glory and Geology', in *The British Journal for the History of Science* 10 (1977), 36–60.

10.  *Treatise on the Deluge*, 2nd edn., 43–60.

11.  Ibid., 10, 65–74, 88.

12.  Ibid., 3, 86–91, Part 3 (247 seq.) passim.

13.  Cf. Bruno von Freyberg, *Johann Gottlob Lehmann*, Erlangen, 1955, esp. 104–15.

14.  Johann Gottlob Lehmann, *Versuch einer Geschichte von Floetz-Gebürgen*, Berlin, 1756, 84–5.

15.  Cf., e.g., Francis C. Haber, *The Age of the World. Moses to Darwin*, Westport, Conn., 1959; Loren Eiseley, *Darwin's Century. Evolution and the Men Who Discovered It*, London, 1959; Stephen Toulmin and June Goodfield, *The Discovery of Time*, London, 1965; Paolo Rossi, *The Dark Abyss of Time* (see Note 3 to Chapter V); Claude C. Albritton, *The Abyss of Time. Changing Conceptions of the Earth's Antiquity after the Sixteenth Century*, San Francisco, 1980.

16.  Robert W.T. Gunther, *Further Correspondence of John Ray*, London, 1928, 260.

17.  William Derham, *Philosophical Letters Between the Late Learned Mr. Ray and Several of his Ingenious Correspondents*, London, 1718, 256.

18.  See pp. 71–72 above.

19.  Cf. Jacques Roger, *Buffon, un philosophe au jardin du roi*, Paris, 1989, 540–1.

20.  Cf. Buffon, *Les Époques de la nature*, V (ie vol. XX of the *Histoire naturelle*), Paris, 1778, 225.

21.  Cf. Eiseley, op. cit., 65 seq.; Toulmin, op. cit., 153 seq.; Rossi, op. cit., 113 seq.

22.  On the sun and death: La Rochefoucauld, *Réflexions morales*, Paris, 1665, maxim 26. The phrase *la sombre abîme du temps* was coined by Buffon.

23.  On Kirwan: Charles C. Gillispie, *Genesis and Geology. A Study in the Relations of Scientific Thought, Natural Theology, and Social Opinion in Great Britain, 1790–1850*, Harvard University Press, 1951, 49 seq. On his life and personality see Michael Donovan, *Biographical Account of the Late Richard Kirwan, Esq.*, Dublin, 1850 (also in *Proceedings of the Royal Irish Academy* 4)

24.  Kirwan, *Geological Essays*, London, 1799, 3.

25.  Ibid., 2–3.

26.  Ibid., 105.

27.  Ibid., 68.

28.  The German explorer and naturalist Peter Simon Pallas believed that the fossils of large tropical animals which he saw in Siberia had been carried there by the same inundation as is described in Genesis and, as he thought, in the documents of many other peoples; but he did not, apparently, regard that inundation as a supernatural event. See his *Observations sur la formation des montagnes, et les changements arrivés à notre globe, pour servir à l'histoire naturelle de M. le Comte de Buffon*, Paris, 1782 (and 1798).

29.  *Geological Essays*, 69.

30.  Ibid., 78–9.

31.  Ibid., 86.

## Chapter 9: Harmonizers

1. On de Luc: Collier, op. cit., 265–81; Gillispie, op. cit., 58 seq.

2. De Luc: *An Elementary Treatise on Geology*, trans. by the author's friend Henry de la Fite, London 1809, vi and 414.

3. De Luc's writings are diffuse. For the gist of the argument see, eg, *Letters on the Physical History of the Earth*, 2nd edn, London, 1831, letter V, 186, 190–6; letter VI, 234–70.

4. Cuvier, trans. Jameson, *Essay on the Theory of the Earth*, Edinburgh, 1817, 171–2.

5. Cf. Nicolaas A. Rupke, *The Great Chain of History: William Buckland and the English School of Geology*, Oxford, Clarendon Press, 1983. Also relevant to this chapter: Charles C. Gillispie, op. cit., chapter 4; Anthony Hallam, *Great Geological Controversies*, 2nd edn., Oxford University Press, 1989, esp. 41 seq.; Richard Huggett, *Cataclysms and Earth History. The Development of Diluvialism*, Oxford, Clarendon Press, 1989, 83 seq.

6. William Tuckwell, *Reminiscences of Oxford*, London, 1900, quoted in Hallam, op. cit., 62.

7. Buckland, *Vindiciae Geologicae*, Oxford, 1820, 23–4.

8. Ibid., 31.

9. *Reliquiae Diluvianae*, 44–7.

10. Ibid., 2nd edn. (1824), 236–7.

11. Sedgwick, 'On diluvial formations', in *Annals of Philosophy*, London, n.s. 10 (1825), 35.

12. Fleming, 'The geological deluge, as interpreted by Baron Cuvier and Professor Buckland, inconsistent with the testimony of Moses and the phenomena of nature', in *Edinburgh New Philosophical Journal* 14 (1826), 205–39.

13. Lyell, *Principles of Geology*, London, 1833–4, vol. 3, 274.

14. Ibid., vol. 4, 149.

15. Sedgwick, 'Presidential Address (1831)' in *Proceedings of the Geological Society of London* 1, 313.

## Chapter 10: Fundamentalists

1. Cf. Rupke, op. cit., 42.

2. On the movement from Granville Penn to John Pye Smith: Milton Millhauser, 'The Scriptural Geologists. An episode in the history of opinion', in *Osiris* 11 (1954) 65–86, esp. 71 seq.

3. Penn, *Comparative Estimate*, 431.

4. Bugg, *Scriptural Geology* II, 351.

5. Ibid., 352–3.

6. Ibid., 355.

7. Ibid., 69.

8. Fairholme, *Physical Demonstration*, 358.

9. Ibid., 423.

10. Representative works: Frederick Nolan, *Analogy of Revelation and Science Established* (1833); Henry Cole, *Popular Geology Subversive of Divine Revelation* (1834); Thomas Gisborne, *Considerations on the Modern Theory of Geology* (1836).

11. John Pye Smith, *Relation*, 242–52. For seventeenth-century precursors see p. 43 above.

12. Kitto's *Cyclopaedia* vol. 1, 54–5.

13. Cunningham Geikie, *Hours with the Bible*, New York, 1886, vol. 1, 169.

14. Whitcomb and Morris, *The Genesis Flood*, 73–4.

15. E.g. Howard M. Teeple, *The*

*Noah's Ark Nonsense*, Evanston, Ill-inois, 1978.

16. The following owes much to the work by Teeple (see preceding note) and to Lloyd R. Bailey, *Noah. The Person and the Story in History and Tradition*, University of South Carolina Press, 1989. Some works by 'ark-believers' include useful surveys of the historical sources; e.g. John War-wick Montgomery, *The Quest for Noah's Ark*, Minneapolis, 1972.

17. Faustus of Byzantium, *History of Armenia*, chapter 10. This work, written some time between 350 and 450 CE, is in Armenian. In the German translation by M. Lauer (Cologne, 1879), the relevant passage is at pp. 17–18. However, it seems that Faustus was thinking of quite a different mountain in quite a different region, and that it was only in the late middle ages that the legend became attached to Mount Ararat; cf. Bailey, op. cit., 73–9, and Appendices 1 and 2, 190–6.

18. Adam Olearius, *The Voyages and Travells*, London, 1669, Book IV, 139 (trans. from the German 1645–47).

19. Jan Janzoon Struys, *The Voiages and Travels*, London, 1684, chapter 18, 212–18.

20. Montgomery, op. cit., 292, 305 seq.

21. Fernand Navarra, *J'ai trouvé l'arche de Noé*, Paris, 1956; *Noah's Ark, I Touched It*, Plainfield, N.J. (or *The Noah's Ark Expedition*, London and Eastbourne).

22. Lloyd R. Bailey, op. cit., 92–114; *idem*, 'Wood from Mount Ararat: Noah's Ark?', in *The Biblical Archaeologist* 40 (1977), 137–46.

23. Cf. Bailey, op. cit., Appendix 4,

203–6. For an impressive piece of fiction on this theme see chap-ter 9 of Julian Barnes, *The History of the World in 10½ Chapters*, Lon-don, 1989.

## Chapter 11: Hidden Meanings Again

1. On the origins of that vogue see Burton Feldman and Robert D. Richardson, *The Rise of Modern Mythology, 1680–1860*, especially the articles on, and quotations from, Jacob Bryant, George Stanley Faber and Charles Dupuis.

2. *Encyclopaedia Biblica*, vol. 1, cols. 1058–9. Zimmern repeated his argument in the revised version of Eberhard Schrader, *Die Keilinschriften und das Alte Testa-ment*, Berlin, 1903, 554 seq. The eminent German classicist Hermann Usener also adopted the solar interpretation in *Die Sintflutsagen*, Bonn, 1899, and in a communication to Karl Dilthey in 1901, repr. in *Kleine Schriften*, vol. 4, Leipzig and Berlin, 1913, 382–96.

3. Ernst Böklen, 'Die Sintflutsage. Versuch einer neuen Erklärung', in *Archiv für Religionswissenschaft* 6, Tübingen and Leipzig, 1903, 1–61, 97–150.

4. *Religions* 29 (1939), 11–12. Reprinted in Dundes, *The Flood Myth*, University of California Press, 1988, 75–85.

5. Otto Rank, 'Die Symbol-schichtung im Wecktraum und ihre Wiederkehr im mythischen Denken', in *Jahrbuch für psycho-analytische und psychopathologische Forschungen* 4 (1912), 51–115,

esp. 107–11. The yearbook was published by Freud and Bleuler and edited by Jung.

6. Forty years after Rank a similar interpretation was advanced by the psychoanalyst and anthropologist Geza Roheim; see extracts in Dundes, op. cit., 151–65.

7. Eleanor Bertine, 'The Great Flood,' in *Jung's Contribution to Our Time: The Collected Papers of Eleanor Bertine*, New York, 1967, 182–208. The passage quoted is at pp. 203–4. The essay was first published in 1944.

8. Alan Dundes, 'The Flood as male myth of creation', in Dundes, op. cit., 167–82. The passages quoted are at pp. 170, 178.

*Appendix*

1. Croft, *Some Animadversion upon a Book intituled the Theory of the Earth*, Preface.

2. Ibid., 70.

3. Keill, *An Examination . . .*, 5.

4. Ibid., 19.

5. Ibid., 21.

6. Ibid., 26.

7. Ibid., 30, 32.

8. Ibid., 178–9, 203.

9. Cf. the check-list in Macklem, *The Anatomy of the World*, 97–8 (see Note 3 to Chapter 5). Also Ernest Tuveson, 'Swift and the World-Makers', in *Journal of the History of Ideas* 11 (1950), 54–74.

10. On the controversy as it developed on the Continent see Rossi, chapter 13 (see Note 3 to Chapter 5.)

# Index

Abich, Hermann 128
Abyss, watery
    in Genesis 44
    in Kircher 44–6
    in Burnet 53–4
    in Steno 77–8
    in Woodward 82
    in Catcott 98
Agassiz, Louis 119
Ambrose, St 30
Ararat, kingdom and
  mountain 12, 126–8
Arbuthnot, John 86
Ark
    Mesopotamian precursors
      of 5, 15
    in Genesis 12
    as 'type' of Church 28–30
    in *Genesis Rabbah* 33–4
    as described by
      Origen 38
    as described by Alfonso
      Tostado 38
    as described by Buteo 40
    in Burnet 55

attempts to find 126–8
*Atrahasis Epic* 3–7
    critical of gods 6–7
    and Genesis 15, 18
Augustine, St 28–9, 30–1

Baptism
    compared with Flood
      30–1
    Anglican rite of 30
Beaumont, John 100
Bertine, Eleanor 132
Böklen, Ernst 131
Browne, Thomas 42
Buckland, William 113–19,
    121, 122
Buffon, George Louis Leclerc,
  Comte de 101, 103, 123
Bugg, George 122–3
Burnet, Thomas 48–61
    his explanation of the
      Flood 54–5
    on the primordial earth
      54
    on mountains 49, 55–6

on the oceans 56
on the end-time 56–7
and Descartes 58–9
on God's curse on the
    earth 59
his reputation and
    influence 60–1
criticisms of 134–6
Burton, Robert 141
Buteo, Johannes 40–1

Cambridge University 48, 83
Catcott, Alexander 97–8
Clement of Rome 24
Croft, Herbert 134
Cuvier, Georges 82, 111–13,
    121, 122, 123

de Luc, Jean-André 109–11
Descartes, René 58–9, 62
Deucalion 8–9
dove, Noah's 5, 12, 15, 31,
    118
Dundes, Alan 132–3

Enki, Mesopotamian god 4–7
Enlil, Mesopotamian god 3–7
Exile, Babylonian 17

Fairholme, George 123–4
Fleming, John 118
Follansbee, Eleanor 131
Frazer, James 131

*Genesis Rabbah* 32–7
on ante-diluvian state
    32–3
on dimensions of ark
    33–4

on animals in ark 34–7
*Gilgamesh, Epic of* 3, 5
discovery of by George
    Smith 20–1
glacial theory 113, 119
Goodman, Godfrey 59–60

Halley, Edmund 69–72, 101
Hutton, James 102–4, 129
Huxley, Thomas 78

Irenaeus, St 26

Jeremiah 17
John Chrysostom, St 29–30
Justin Martyr 25

Keill, John 135–6
Kircher, Athanasius 44–6
Kirchmaier, George 43
Kirwan, Richard 104–7, 129

Latitudinarians 48
La Peyrère, Isaac 43
Lehmann, Johann Gottlob
    98–9
Lhwydd, Edward 100
Lyell, Charles 118, 123

Matthew, Gospel of 23–4
Montgomery, John Warwick
    128
More, Henry 48
Morris, Henry M. 125–6

Navarra, Fernand 128
Newton, Isaac 47, 61, 62, 63,
    65, 82, 102
Nisir, Mount 126

Noah
　in Genesis 11–14
　typological interpretation
　　of 24–6
　as 'type' of Christ 25–6
　in *Genesis Rabbah* 33,
　　35–6
　in medieval speculation
　　38, 40

Olearius, Adam 127
Origen 25–6, 28
Ovid, on story of Deucalion
　8–9
Oxford University 113–16

Parrot, Johann Friedrich
　Wilhelm 127
Penn, Granville 121–3
Peter, Second Letter of 24,
　48, 56
phoenix 35, 41
Price, George McCready 124

Raleigh, Walter 44
Rank, Otto 131–2
raven, Noah's 6, 12, 15, 31,
　35–6
Ray, John 85, 100
Revelation, Book of 56, 57

Scheuchzer, Johann Jakob
　87–92
　on marine fossils 88–9
　on supposedly human
　　fossils 89–92
Segwick, Adam 113, 117
Shurrupak, ancient
　Mesopotamian town 1

Smith, George 19–21
Smith, John Pye 124
Steno (Niels Stensen) 74–8
　on *glossopetrae* 75
　on stratification 76
　and Descartes 76–7
　on the Flood 78
Struys, Jan Jansoon 127

Tertullian 73
Theophilus of Antioch 24,
　94–6
typology
　defined 23
　applied to Flood 23–31
　and allegory 26

universality of Flood
　questioned
　　in seventeenth century 43
　　in nineteenth century
　　　124
Ussher, James 95

Vossius (Voss), Isaak 43

Warren, Erasmus 134
Whiston, William 48, 62–9
　and Cambridge University
　　62–3
　his explanation of the
　　Flood 67–8
　on the primordial earth
　　66–7
　on the post-diluvial world
　　68
　on the end-time 69
　on Burnet 65
　his reputation and

influence 63–4
criticisms of 135–7
Whitcome, John C. 125–6
Woodward, John 79–86
   his explanation of the
     Flood 82–3
   on the consequences of
     the Flood 83–5

and Burnet 86
and Steno 83
criticisms of 85–6

Zimmern, Heinrich 130
Ziusdra, Ziusudra,
   Mesopotamian Flood hero
   2, 126

JAN 2 4 1997

222.1106 Cohn, Norman Rufus
COH          Colin.

        Noah's flood.

$25.00

| DATE | | |
|---|---|---|
| | | |
| | | |
| | | |
| | | |
| | | |
| | | |
| | | |
| | | |
| | | |
| | | |
| | | |
| | | |

LAD ND (8)                    5/09
LAD nd (8)                    12/22

PLAINVIEW OLD BETHPAGE PUBLIC LIBRARY
999 OLD COUNTRY ROAD
PLAINVIEW, N.Y. 11803

BAKER & TAYLOR